ALSO BY ANITA DIAMANT

Good Harbor

The Red Tent

The New Jewish Wedding

*How to Be a Jewish Parent: A Practical Handbook
for Family Life*

*Saying Kaddish: How to Comfort the Dying,
Bury the Dead, and Mourn as a Jew*

*Choosing a Jewish Life: A Guidebook for People Converting to
Judaism and for Their Family and Friends*

*Bible Baby Names: Spiritual Choices from
Judeo-Christian Tradition*

*The New Jewish Baby Book: Names, Ceremonies, and Customs—
a Guide for Today's Families*

*Living a Jewish Life: Jewish Traditions, Customs, and
Values for Today's Families*

PITCHING MY TENT

*On Marriage, Motherhood,
Friendship, and Other Leaps of Faith*

ANITA DIAMANT

SCRIBNER
New York   London   Toronto   Sydney   Singapore

SCRIBNER
1230 Avenue of the Americas
New York, NY 10020

First Scribner trade paperback edition 2005

SCRIBNER and design are trademarks of
Macmillan Library Reference USA, Inc., used under license
by Simon & Schuster, the publisher of this work.

For information about special discounts for bulk purchases,
please contact Simon & Schuster Special Sales:
1-800-456-6798 or business@simonandschuster.com

"This Is Just to Say" by William Carlos Williams, from *Collected Poems:
1909–1939, Volume I* © 1938 by New Directions Publishing Corp. Reprinted
by permission of New Directions Publishing Corp.
Portions of this book have appeared in *The Boston Globe Magazine*,
Parenting magazine, and JewishFamily.com

Designed by Kyoko Watanabe
Text set in Walbaum

Manufactured in the United States of America

1   3   5   7   9   10   8   6   4   2

The Library of Congress has cataloged the Scribner edition as follows:
Diamant, Anita.
Pitching my tent: on marriage, motherhood, friendship, and
other leaps of faith /Anita Diamant.
p. cm.
1. Diamant, Anita—Anecdotes. 2. Jewish women—United States—
Anecdotes. 3. Jews—United States—Anecdotes. 4. Judaism—United States.
I. Title.

E184.37.D53A3 2003
296.7—dc21
2003045440

ISBN-13: 978-0-7432-4616-3
ISBN-10: 0-7432-4616-0
ISBN-13: 978-0-7432-4617-0 (Pbk)
ISBN-10: 0-7432-4617-9 (Pbk)

CONTENTS

CONTENTS

CONTENTS

CONTENTS

HOME FOR THE SOUL

INTRODUCTION

Before *The Red Tent*, before *Good Harbor*, before and during six books on contemporary Jewish life, I was a columnist.

I wrote essays about friendship and fashion, about marriage and electoral politics, about abortion, lingerie, situation comedies, birth, death, God, country, and my dog. I covered the waterfront and the supermarket, my synagogue, the waiting room outside the intensive care unit, and my own kitchen table.

I did this over the course of twenty years for publications that included a weekly newspaper with a mostly twenty-something readership, and later for a Sunday-magazine audience of millions. I wrote for food lovers in a New

England magazine, for the parents of young children in a national publication, and for an international Jewish audience in an on-line magazine. Most of the time, my assignment was weekly; sometimes, it was monthly.

My job was to report on the events of the day and the changes under my own roof. The challenge was to pay closer-than-average attention and then shape my experiences and reactions into entertaining prose that rose above the level of my own navel. It was more than a great job— it was a meaningful job.

This collection, culled from those publications and years, turns out to be a sort of diary. It includes musings about the contents of my refrigerator as well as reflections about the most important decisions of my life. To divorce and marry again. To have a child. To live a Jewish life.

I suppose it's a measure of how much the world has changed that what once seemed like "edgy" choices now seem fairly mainstream. But at the time, I was thinking and doing things that were simply unimaginable for women at any other period in human history. Having been born female, white, and middle class in the United States, in the middle of the twentieth century, meant the women's movement happened to me, in me, for me. It meant that it was highly unlikely that I would die in childbirth, and it meant that I could teach my daughter to speak in her own voice. It meant I could love my work and love my family. And it meant that there was an audience for what I had to say about the trials and joys of this girl's life.

Actually, the audience was the great, unexpected gift of the assignment because they wrote back. A few said, "No way," and "How dare you?" But many more said, "Me, too," and "Thanks."

We connected—my readers and I—because we were trying something entirely new. We were not just tinkering around the edges, adjusting our "roles" as women and men. We were reinventing the female psyche and soul, which of course required a radical recasting of the male. We're still at it, too, and with more confidence, wisdom, and resources every year. That our daughters and sons are blasé about this transformation is a measure of our success.

Looking back through these essays, reflecting on the reflections, is a lot like leafing through the family photo album. I stop and exclaim over the difference between my daughter then (kindergarten) and my daughter now (college). The changes in me are not quite as photogenic, but I think I've become kinder and more patient. I sure hope so.

My tent is filled with friends and songs and books and memories. My tent—and I hope yours, too—is filled with blessings. Come see.

LOVE, MARRIAGE,
BABY CARRIAGE

I'M NOT on this journey alone. I travel with Mr. Jim Ball, magazine pack rat, teller of jokes, sweetheart, catalyst. Our falling in love was a beginning for so much, including my own religious journey.

Of course, Jim didn't bargain for the prominent role he would eventually play in my writing. But he didn't object, either. If he had, you wouldn't be reading these pages. Whenever an essay about Jim was published, readers would ask me (actually, they'd sidle up to me and whisper), "Is he okay with this?" And he was. He vetted every word and often encouraged me to include a funnier detail that I'd thought too personal to mention. He's that kind of guy. Lucky me.

THE KISS

EVERY FRIDAY NIGHT, I kiss my husband. No matter how tired we are. No matter what dreadful things we said to each other earlier in the day. No matter what. The kiss is neither perfunctory nor passionate. And yet, even when there are six other people in the room, it is intimate.

All week long, a kiss is just a kiss. But our Friday-night kiss is something else. It acknowledges a connection that is ultimately as mysterious as any sunset, as sacred as any psalm.

This is a ritual kiss. It takes place in the dining room, immediately after we light two new, white candles and sing the blessing that marks the beginning of Shabbat, the

Jewish Sabbath. Candles and kiss are followed by blessings over wine and bread.

I didn't grow up with this kind of ceremony. My parents were not religiously observant at home and we didn't belong to a synagogue until I was in junior high school, so I had little formal religious education. But my parents survived the Holocaust in Europe, and Yiddish was one of the languages spoken at my house. I never had any doubts about my ethnic or religious identity; still, it was only when I fell in love with a lapsed Presbyterian and began to think of us as a family-to-be that I realized how important it was to me that any child of mine know that she was Jewish.

Jim had no problem with raising our hypothetical offspring within my tradition. The problem was that I didn't know enough about Judaism to pass it along to another generation. So, with my gentile boyfriend willingly in tow, I started my remedial religious education and recovered my spiritual birthright. Jim and I joined a Jewish reading group and began attending Sabbath services. When we started shopping around for a rabbi to officiate at our wedding, Jim decided to convert to Judaism.

We both attended the intro class offered by the Reform movement, and we met regularly with Rabbi Lawrence Kushner, who remains our teacher and dear friend. In the process, Jim and I had the pleasure of being students together. We read books, discussed Rabbi Kushner's questions as we drove home from our sessions with him, and started lighting candles on Friday night.

Jim's conversion curriculum was part of my Jewish education, too, including a survey course with a hundred other people, and my first attempt at learning Hebrew. And as we began to plan our wedding, I was amazed by the joyous wisdom of Jewish ritual, and found the idea for my first book. Along the way, Jim and I joined a synagogue, which, it turns out, is just about the only public venue where we are identified and known as Anita-and-Jim, the couple.

Like most other married folks we know, Jim and I live discrete lives. We lunch and gossip with different colleagues, we never serve on the same volunteer committees, we sometimes go to the movies separately. On weekends, we often end up running errands on opposite ends of town.

But at temple, we sit side by side, holding hands, nodding at sermons, singing in unison, sighing in prayer. If I show up for a service by myself, people are quick to ask where Jim is.

At one point when Jim was laid off from a job—in a particularly nasty and abrupt way—I insisted we go to Shabbat services. As soon as our bad news got around, we were surrounded by faces registering concern and reassurance. There were offers of help and support, not just for each of us individually but for both of us. "We know how tough this can be," we were told by other couples who'd been through it.

For Jim and me, religious ritual and affiliation are mainstays of our marriage. Hanging in our bedroom is a *ketubah*—the Jewish marriage contract we signed at our wedding. It's a romantic reminder of one of the best days of our life together, but it's also a legal document, a black-and-white (and red and blue and gold and green) testament to our commitment.

I feel very lucky—blessed is really a better word—about this particular aspect of our relationship. Religion is so often a loaded subject for couples. Questions of faith and religious practice can unleash yearning, misunderstanding, anger, pain—sometimes separation and divorce. Couples can find it even more difficult to talk about religion than about sex or money.

This silence reflects the American notion that religion is a strictly private matter. It's a view that helps contain intolerance and also abolished most taboos against interfaith marriages, but it tends to paper over profound spiritual differences within relationships. Even when couples share the same religious background, questions like "Do you belong to a church?" or "Are you going to send your kids to Sunday school?" can stir up unforeseen conflicts: She's nostalgic for the community of her youth, while he remembers nothing but hypocrisy and boredom. He thinks it's essential that the family attend church on Sunday; she feels that spending a day in the woods is much more spiritually uplifting.

Couples get divorced over issues of faith. In some cases, religious differences reflect dissimilar personalities. The person who wants to join a church may be someone who thrives in groups, while the spouse who has no interest in affiliating feels overwhelmed by them. But most couples starting out are unaware of the significance that religious choices can have on their marriage over time. Even people who explore the subject before they marry often don't have any idea of what the impact will be—especially if and when children get added to the mix.

Jim and I certainly had no idea how important a shared religious life would be when we first got married and had all the time in the world for each other. After a few years, we were routinely forgetting to tell each other what we did all day, who we saw, how we felt. The Jewish calendar works as our emotional clock, reminding us to reconnect as we follow ritual cycles synchronized to the week, the year, and our unfolding lives.

During the annual observance of the High Holidays— the Jewish New Year and the Day of Atonement—the liturgy includes an admonition to ask forgiveness of all the people you have wronged during the previous year. Since we inevitably do the most damage to the people we love the most, Jim and I turn to each other and apologize. It's pretty humbling to enumerate and confess the pettiness, rudeness, thoughtlessness, and occasional cruelties of our married life. But we forgive each other and we resolve to try harder, knowing full well that next year we will face each other to make the same amends.

And then there is our Friday-night kiss.

Our daughter, Emilia, has seen this kiss ever since she was born. Over the years—as a baby in our arms, as a four-year-old standing on a chair between us, as a teenager with friends in tow—she has watched us embrace. When she was little, I could see how it reassured her. It reassures us, too, especially after a rocky week.

From the beginning of our marriage to last Friday night, Jim and I have stopped the clock to see, smell, taste, and touch what's right with the world and with our life together. We offer prayers for food and drink, light and life. We create a little island of peace. We kiss. We say, Amen.

RELIGIOUS FANATICS

IF I LET IT SLIP in casual conversation that the Friday-night meal in my house begins with blessings over candles, wine, and a braided loaf of bread, I risk the following response: First, the eyebrows ascend into the hairline. Then the eyes narrow slightly, telegraphing surprise, even alarm. You? Religious? But you seem so, well, normal.

When it comes out that I not only do Jewish stuff at home but am an active synagogue member and have written ten books about contemporary Jewish practice, nostrils flare, searching out a telltale whiff of cant or self-righteousness. Or I'm asked if *The New Jewish Wedding* and *How to Be a Jewish Parent* are humor books.

One man, who was stunned by these revelations, bombarded me with a list of questions, aimed at finding out the precise extent of my fanaticism. "You mean, if someone gave you tickets, you wouldn't go out to see a play on Friday night? How often do you go to services? Does your daughter attend public school?"

But when I told him that I did not keep one set of china for meat dishes and another for dairy, he relaxed. For that particular secular Jew, the litmus test for authentic religious Judaism is the willingness to forever forgo spaghetti carbonara, which contains not only pork but cream as well. While I was still a curiosity, a throwback, at least, I had ceased being a threat. Because I do not keep that kind of a kosher home, I was not, by his lights, entirely serious.

A woman I met in Texas would agree with that assessment, though for diametrically different reasons. She told me plainly that she would not permit my Jewish books in her home because they might give her children the wrong ideas. I understood her point since nearly every page affirms the existence of more than one authentically Jewish choice for everything from the contents of a marriage contract to the contents of one's refrigerator. My kitchen would have been proof positive to the lady from the Lone Star State that I was not to be taken seriously.

It's striking how the messages from the left and from the right are so similar: either you are strictly kosher (according to an Orthodox interpretation) or you are not really Jewish at all. Either you fall in line behind the pope or you are not a good Catholic. Either you take the Gospels literally or you are not a genuine Christian. Either you embrace some brand of orthodoxy or the authenticity of your religious belief, practice, and identity is suspect.

One of my friends is circumspect about her profound faith and identity as a Christian because, as she puts it, people immediately assume she is a "Falwellian," someone who has ceded her cerebral cortex in exchange for the smug certainty of a berth on the other side. And yet, within the walls of her mainline Protestant church, she is viewed as something of a radical, if not exactly a heretic, for her insistence that the congregation take a stand on such worldly issues as hunger in the cities and injustice in the hemisphere.

There are countless examples of nonorthodox piety thriving within the American landscape, though they rarely make the nightly news. When it comes to the subject of faith, the media continue to be fascinated with monks and nuns of the strictest orders, children who become so devout they will not eat in their parents' homes, denominations that banish gay sons and lesbian daughters.

It is never easy explaining how or why one chooses to acknowledge the holy or to express radical awe. But the added awkwardness of being nonorthodox *and* a serious Jew, Catholic, or Protestant owes a lot to romantic fantasies about religious life in the past: *Once upon a time the churches were full to bursting every Sunday. In the good old days, no Jew ever touched a plate of spaghetti carbonara.* But then the evils of modernity (such as birth control) erased that communal state of grace, and now we're stuck with a world-class mess of doubt, alienation, women in the pulpit, too many questions, too many choices.

Some people find refuge from the contemporary fray in received authority. I relish my freedom to wrestle with my faith, respectful of the sustaining traditions of the past and grateful for the insights and wisdom of the present. I agree that nothing is simple anymore. And for that, I thank God.

WHY MARRY?

I HAD JUST TURNED twenty the first time I got married, and that was not so much a decision as a convenient and comfortable acquiescence to two eager families. It wasn't anything like a shotgun wedding, nor did the pressure come out of concern for appearances. Our parents wanted us to marry so that they could be unequivocal in their support for their already-living-together children, and so they could be part of each other's families, too. They all seemed certain that our marriage was a good idea, but I wasn't so sure. One of my friends recalls that, about ten minutes before the wedding ceremony, I was joking about escape clauses and hatches, "just in case."

My nervousness was as much a cultural marker as a personal panic. It was 1975 and none of my friends or classmates had gotten married yet. At the time, it seemed a pretty dubious option. Marriage was seen as a symptom of patriarchy, with supporting evidence provided by actuarial charts and domestic violence reports. The 50 percent divorce rate seemed to argue for keeping love free from the workings of the State. (That's how people talked in the mid-seventies.)

Family pressure trumped our politics, so we got married and stayed that way for seven years. It went from good to no longer good to what-exactly-are-we-doing? For most of that time, I avoided telling people I was married because I wasn't exactly sure why I was.

I suppose I could chalk up my malaise to having been too young to make such an enormous decision. Of course, lots of people get married even younger and sometimes those couples make it, forever after. The other half of that statistic doesn't stop anyone from trying. The numbers remain amazingly consistent: most people spend some part of their adult lives legally wed, and the vast majority of divorced people will try it again.

I don't believe the urge has much to do with our genes. Studies and theories that attempt to explain monogamy with analogies to swans and chimpanzees just make me giggle. Bird and monkey couples don't plan for retirement, don't try to change each other's habits, don't know their mothers' maiden names. Nor are the animal records rife with male birds or monkeys who kill their mates.

Marriage is a powerful cultural tropism with lousy odds. Because no matter how amicable, no matter how little community property, any divorce is a trauma. The way a broken collarbone is a trauma.

I'd been through that once, so when Jim fell in love with the older/wiser me, I needed an answer to the question Why marry? Why risk it again, especially since living together was working out just fine?

The prospect of parenthood certainly contributed to our decision to tie the knot. If I was ever going to head down that irrevocable road (I was thirty and looking ahead), I wanted a trustworthy associate, for all the conventional social, economic, and ergonomic reasons. Jim seemed to be the perfect candidate: easygoing, patient, a great goofball around babies. And besides, I was nuts about him.

So I did it. And I did have an answer to the question this time, though it barely addresses the biology, sociology, or even the social conventions of marriage.

Why marry?

Because marriage publicly affirms the possibility of moving toward another person without reservation. With that momentum, we are propelled toward the center of the heart, toward the center of the universe, and however far that gets us is farther than we'd otherwise go alone.

Why marry?

Because every wedding enacts a personal connection to the universal story of the human hope for wholeness. Because by stepping into the hyperbarically charged space on the altar (in front of the priest, under the canopy), the bride and groom join in a dance that goes all the way back to the beginning of memory.

Getting married is an attempt at turning air into matter, transforming the ineffable workings of the heart into things that are "real": the invitation, the dress, the ring. The words that constitute a wedding are magical incantations of the highest order. In the presence of witnesses and voiced by a vested authority, two people are pronounced a single unit. Ta-da!

And by the way, the legal arguments for extending the marriage franchise to queer couples simply acknowledge that gay men and lesbians are members of the human family, complete with photographers, caterers, and the challenge of juggling Thanksgiving between two families of origin.

Every wedding is an invocation of peace and wholeness and connection and joy. Good wishes flow from family and friends, through history and community, with wings and prayers and everything that might turn out to be holy in the universe.

So that's why Jim and I got married—to receive that shower of blessings, hoping with all our hearts to make them last.

BLAST OFF

WE'D BEEN TOGETHER for five years when our daughter was born. We had survived planning a wedding, vacations, job changes, and sharing a tiny bathroom. We had developed a conjugal rhythm for walking, shopping, and going to the movies; I got the seats, he got the eats. He stopped buying polyester, I stopped telegraphing the punch lines of his jokes.

We had each other figured out pretty well. Then we became parents, and from the minute we arrived at the hospital, things between us changed, profoundly and forever.

Having a child turned up the volume in our relationship. Our marriage, which had been so comfortable, so figured out, suddenly acquired an edge. With Emilia's birth, we went from cruising a country lane at thirty-five miles per hour while chatting agreeably about the tune on the radio to tearing up the straightaway 150—and forget the small talk. Having a baby meant we weren't just playing house anymore. The newlyweds, the young couple, moved out. The grown-ups arrived, and they were us.

We first met this new incarnation of ourselves in the labor and delivery unit of Beth Israel Hospital in Boston, which was for us the Holy of Holies, where being and not-being intersected, where we spent a day and a half holding on to each other for dear life.

Even in the age of technological medicine, the journey from the womb to the world is frightening. And not just for the stranger within. Jim and I were unprepared for what this trip would do to us, two amusement park wimps for whom even the Ferris wheel is too scary. When giving birth began to look like the mother of all roller-coaster rides, we realized that we were going to be tested. Would we throw up in each other's laps? Would we pretend to be brave? Would we respect each other in the morning?

Let's get one thing straight. Jim was not my "coach." What a stupid thing to call someone who takes you into the bathroom to pee, who holds you around the waist in the shower, who stands next to you in the operating room and never takes his eyes from your face. Throughout labor and delivery, I kept telling him, "I'm glad you're with me, whoever you are."

After thirty-six hours and a cesarean section, we found each other, and the news was good. I could take it. Which is to say, I could relinquish control. (Not that I had much choice.) And Jim became the man of my dreams. He had sweated empathy and told me everything that I wanted to hear while the nurses nodded appreciatively. We professed our love to each other a thousand times, and every time it was a revelation. Talk about foxhole conversations. Talk about bonding.

When we finally met our baby in the glare of the operating room, everyone said she was beautiful, but in my drugged haze I could only be vaguely grateful for the news that she had all her parts. And at that moment, I wasn't overwhelmed with maternal love for the little bundle in the improbably cute hospital cap. I was curious about her, but in truth, I only had eyes for the bedraggled, unshaven, exhausted man staring, mooning, at the swaddled thing they put into his arms.

Later, in my hospital room as we gazed at each other above her sleeping head, we loved each other like survivors of a shipwreck. We loved each other with the adrenaline of a basketball team that had just won the NBA championship after a dozen dry seasons. When Jim and I first became lovers, we gave our emotional address as "Sky City, USA." What a kick to find ourselves back up there.

Of course, the intensity of labor and delivery quickly faded into the shadowy twilight of the Fourth Trimester, the hormone-driven first months of motherhood. As soon as we got home, we forgot about each other altogether. The relationship that used to be a two-way street disappeared into the now visible center of the universe, our daughter, the world's most wonderful child.

Every now and then I would get cranky about not being Jim's only baby-oh-baby anymore. But I simultaneously relegated him to being the low man on the family's ever-heavier totem pole of needs. In my powerful role as the nursing, on-leave mother, I began to feel and act like the expert parent, dismissing Jim's intuitions and efforts. I whined and issued edicts. He sulked and occasionally slammed a door.

During those first few months, our discontents and tensions were generally eclipsed by our shared adoration of Emilia. Jim and I both wanted a baby girl, and when we got what we wanted, we lost each other in her.

Slowly, we regained our footing and encountered each other again. Or perhaps I should say that we found two people named Mommy and Daddy, with whom we were not fully comfortable.

Things between us had become charged, heightened. Everything mattered more. Trivial arguments assumed dark, ominous proportions. What if this stupid spat about orange juice, her bedtime, his magazines, my coffee, never ends and we get divorced and Emilia becomes a statistic? The stakes were so high and we were so exhausted.

The first time she spiked a fever, we shrieked uncontrollably at each other about what to do. Heading for the doctor's office, we bit our tongues, pale with worry about her and horrified at the things we'd said to each other.

No cause for alarm, the doctor said.

At home, we put her in the crib. Then we kissed and made up, in an embrace that turned out to be as passionate as it was tender. We were going to have to figure out how to be married to each other all over again.

The fact that Jim and I had shared the most awe-filled hours of our lives reshuffled the cards we had been dealt by our own parents. All the expectations about what mothers do and what fathers don't do were officially up for grabs, and I don't just mean whose turn it was to feed, or change, or do the midnight ramble with an inconsolable baby.

We were not the same people anymore. Strong and unfamiliar currents of passion and anger drew us together and pushed us apart. We were more tentative and tense with each other than ever before. But we were also closer, because of what we had learned under fire: that we owed each other the best parts of ourselves. That we were stronger together than we were apart. That, in the clutch, we could count on each other for the amazing grace that is unconditional love.

NAGGING

I PROMISED JIM THAT if he quit smoking, I would never nag him about anything else—ever. "Give up the cigarettes," I said, "and I swear I'll never complain that the top of your bureau looks like a garbage dump. You'll never hear another word out of me about the money you spend on computer programs or designer socks. I won't bug you about taking out the compost or buying the wrong brand of toilet paper."

Jim didn't believe me. He is convinced that it would take a total personality transplant to stop me from nagging. And he may be right. After all, I was trained by a champion. My mother can nag about the organization of an underwear drawer and the placement of garbage cans and the use of salt.

"I'm not that bad, am I?" I ask.

"No, you're not that bad," he says, wisely. But we both know I'm bad enough.

I nag about clutter, unmade beds, incomplete check registers, sloppily hung clothes, and lots of other stuff.

Does Jim nag back? Well, he does get on my case for not refrigerating beverages promptly, but that's about it. In our marriage, I am the nagger, Jim is the nagee.

I am not proud of this state of affairs. I know that nagging is about as attractive as spitting, and when I hear my daughter echoing my complaints about Jim's clutter, I shrink in horror at the idea that I'm responsible for another generation of nagging. It's a crummy legacy.

Sometimes I worry that my nagging is like water on a rock, with my *drip, drip, drip* of disapproval eating away at a solid relationship. And then I stop—or, to be more precise, I pause. In my more rational moments, I understand that nagging is not only unattractive but also a total waste of energy. Jim is never going to (a) clear out his piles of magazines, (b) pinch pennies, or (c) give his lungs and heart a break from nicotine just because of anything I say. And say. And say.

I take some cold comfort in the fact that nagging is a part of virtually every other marriage I know of. My friend S. says, "I'm still nagging T. about stuff I've been nagging him about for nine years. Why don't I just give it up?"

But S. won't be giving it up anytime soon since most of her nagging revolves around household chores. "The way I see it, we both have two jobs, but I'm the only one who knows it. So nagging is my way of reminding T. that he's got this other job, too, which includes loading his dirty dishes directly into the dishwasher." With a laugh and a sigh, she concludes, "The only way I'll stop nagging is by getting a staff of seven domestic servants."

A large proportion of my nagging focuses on household tasks, too, which means that the potential for nagging is actually higher in my marriage than it was for my parents. My mother never expected my father to cook the family dinner or iron his son's shirts. I, on the other hand, do expect Jim to cook, clean, and be a fully engaged parent. So in addition to demanding, "Why can't you ever mow the lawn without my asking you to?" I also have to know, "How come you don't know the name of Emilia's art teacher and I do?"

I used to believe that nagging was a sex-linked attribute. Men tend to go bald, women nag. But then I met a profoundly role-reversed couple. On their first date, she was the one who informed him that she wasn't going to change to suit him and warned him not to try. He's the cook (she can barely scramble an egg), and, by her cheerful admission, he is a far more fastidious housekeeper. He is also the one who tapped his watch with exasperation when their three-year-old's nap schedule was in danger of being thrown off one sultry summer afternoon. "If he doesn't sleep soon, dinner and then the whole evening will be shot," he said. Actually, he said that three times.

The four of us were eating lunch and ruefully confessing our complaining habits, when Jim stepped away to light a cigarette. The nagging male, who happens to be a physician, sighed at the sight and said, "There's something tragic about nagging on behalf of a good cause."

There is, of course, an obvious difference between haranguing your spouse in the hope of preventing cancer and bugging him about the purchase of yet another pair of brown socks. But, ultimately, all nagging seems to be equally futile. Then again, maybe nagging functions as a sort of marital safety valve, a way to vent everyday annoyances and disappointments so they don't build up into destructive explosions.

Whatever it is, I wish I could say that I'd figured out a way to stop or at least cut down. I wish I could say I'd successfully broken the pattern of marital carping and picking, caviling and fussing. I also wish I could tell you that I'd shed those pesky five pounds and won the lottery.

Alas, none of those things is true. I just hope you don't leave this book lying around and expect somebody else to pick it up and put it where it belongs.

TRUCE AND
CONSEQUENCES

UNCONDITIONAL LOVE lasts among the angels on high, but here on earth, reports from the path of true love sometimes read like dispatches from a demilitarized war zone.

Dateline Boston: An uneasy truce has been declared in a small but ugly conflict that has, on occasion, threatened to erupt into a full-scale war. For the moment, however, white flags are in evidence. My husband stopped smoking.

I ought to be jubilant. The forces of life, love, and cleaner, whiter teeth have triumphed. Where piles of matchbooks once littered the bureau, now there are toothpicks and packs of sugarless gum. I should be dancing around the kitchen. But I am not. I am holding my breath.

All's quiet on the domestic front, but history has taught me sad lessons about nicotine, lying, and love. I feel like a nuclear-arms negotiator bargaining with the devil himself. Every bone in my body aches with suspicion, and I find myself growling, "Verify, verify, verify!"

It all started out so dreamily. The early stages of romance are sort of hazy anyway, but when Jim and I began keeping company, his smoky wreath seemed part of the amorous ambience, like the cloudy fog of a dry-ice machine. The public service campaigns had not, it seems, totally extinguished my childhood association of cigarettes with passion.

When I was growing up, everybody smoked. My mother's manicured fingers and my father's gentle hands were always busy with cigarettes. All the movie stars smoked, except maybe Doris Day, and I never aspired to wholesomeness. No wonder, then, that I glowed in response when the dark, handsome fellow I would eventually marry lit up.

That vaporous idyll was doomed because it really was love, the kind that comes with consequences, such as the fact that his mortality frightens me more than the combined threat of global warming, ozone depletion, and Amazon deforestation.

The Cloud Nine phase of our relationship did not end with a bang or a whimper, but with a cough. One morning he arose hacking and rattling and making other sounds from the crypt. He didn't know it, but with that *ack-ack* burst, he had fired the first shot. I had no choice but to fight back, not only to defend his life and my happiness, but also to save the united state of US.

I had no doubt of my eventual victory. Surely, I thought, he will stop. Now that he's got me, he doesn't need them anymore. One night, as he lit his third after-dinner cigarette, I asked, "Have you ever thought about giving them up?"

"Sure," he said.

When we got married I asked, "When?"

"Soon," he replied.

I offered to pay for hypnosis, acupuncture, anything that might help him stop. I tried bribes. "If you quit, you can buy a new CD player."

I wheedled. He barked. I glowered. He sulked. None of this is exactly good for a marriage.

The day we brought our daughter home from the hospital, I blubbered, "When?" Teary-eyed, he said, "Now."

I didn't see him smoke a single cigarette for almost a year after that. I ignored the after-dinner trips to "get something" out of the car and I simply pretended not to know. Then someone from work let the cat out of the bag: he was the biggest offender at his officially smoke-free office.

Hostilities recommenced. "Fathers don't drive drunk," I shrieked. "You don't have the right to commit suicide."

I nagged like I never nagged before. I was terrified. So,

of course, was he. Everyone knows what cigarettes do to the heart, lungs, skin, libido, brain.

You might think that our mutual fear would have allied us against a common enemy, but it doesn't work that way with addictions. There is always too much free-floating blame and guilt, and ultimately, only one of us had the power to change things.

It was a standoff. It was awful.

And then, on his birthday, he quit.

The long, dirty war was over, but the consequences lingered. The fight had defined our identities: cop and robber, spy and double agent. I found myself sneaking out to the hallway to rummage through his pockets, searching for that telltale golden thread encased in plastic, the key to a fresh pack. I sniffed at his sweaters and stuck my nose into the car ashtray.

This is shameful behavior, and I am ashamed, but then, wars leave all kinds of scars. Relapse and renewed fighting are clear and present dangers, and we have walked down this road before.

I watch him warily now. His color is better and his cough diminished. But he is fighting his own daily battle. If he wins, the war between us really will be over.

Will the truce hold for another week? Is this just a momentary lull in the conflict, or will it prove to be a lasting peace? News at six and eleven, tonight and every night.

GRIEF, DISPOSSESSED

THE GRAPEVINE THAT binds me to my first husband grows more tenuous every year. My ex and I share only one mutual friend now, and it was almost in passing that he told me Milton was back in the hospital.

Milton was my father-in-law for seven years. He paid part of my college tuition. He cried when I told him I was going to keep my own family name rather than take his. A father of sons, he hovered and worried over me as his daughter, and like a natural child, I both resented and came to depend upon his attentions. Milton's constitutional coolness never hid his affection for me. To this day, I'm not sure he knew that I loved him, too.

If Milton was in the hospital, I knew that the leukemia had returned, and that the aggressive, debilitating chemotherapy he'd undertaken had bought him less than a year. Before I heard the news of his relapse, I don't think I fully understood the cliché "My heart stopped." The heart doesn't stop at all; what actually happens is a sudden, overwhelming awareness of the noisy ebb and flow that keeps you alive. Far away, a sleeping part of my heart was dying.

The phone rang only once in the Midwestern ranch house. It had been many years since I set the table there, but I still could have drawn the floor plan: four bedrooms, two baths, the chair by the fireplace where Milton liked to relax after a game of tennis.

My ex-husband's wife answered. "This is Anita," I said. She had doubtless fielded dozens of calls that day and she hesitated. "In Boston," I added. And then Milton's first-born son, my first love, told me it was only a matter of days. No, his dad was not in pain. His mother was doing as well as could be expected.

I hung up and dialed my parents to tell them the sad news. I could almost hear their faces crumble.

Milton died the next day.

The years since I had seen my father-in-law were filled with changes: retirement and a new daughter-in-law for him, a new family for me. And between us, a profound silence. I stayed in touch with Ruth, his wife, my first mother-in-law. We exchanged letters and birthday cards, and occasionally talked on the phone. Ruth always conveyed Milton's greetings, but when she spoke of his continuing pride in me, I was as embarrassed as honored. The divorce had deeply hurt all four parents, but Milton was the only one with whom I had let the breakup go unspoken, unacknowledged. After the omission lengthened into years, it never seemed possible for us to talk about anything.

I suppose that, to all appearances, there was no real tie between Milton and me. According to law, custom, and convention, our connection had been severed. He was no longer kin and I could not honestly call him a friend. Yet I was bereaved and my grief had no quarter. I would not be counted as a mourner. There was no prayer for a former daughter-in-law to say.

When I told people of my loss, they said, "I always forget that you were married before." So I wrapped up my mourning in a private bundle and looked at photo albums I hadn't touched in ages.

Crying for Milton, I cried for Ruth, whose loss is immeasurable. And for their son, with whom I did so much growing up. And for the way I once belonged to that family, thicker than water.

I wish I had worn a black armband for Milton, or hung a black cloth in the window, or something. I wish those kinds of symbols had the power they once did, but our time is coldly impatient of death's toll. I am stunned at how people interrupted my reminiscences about Milton's generosity. I didn't want to be distracted from my sadness. I didn't want cheering up. What I wanted was sympathy. But for losses like mine, losses without standing or status, grief is an orphaned state, and lonely. Peace abide him.

AIRING IT OUT

THINGS BETWEEN US were bad. We weren't talking. We weren't kissing. We weren't, well, you know.

It had been like that for months and it was starting to feel normal. Jim's silence didn't help. My yelling didn't help. Courtesy at the dinner table didn't make much difference. We roused ourselves from the dark blue funk to rejoice in our thriving child, who was doing all the miraculous things she was supposed to be doing: walking, talking, laughing, and even sleeping through the night once in a while. But after we tucked her in, the space between us went dead. I had never been so lonely.

"That's it," I said finally. "Either we go see a counselor . . . or else."

I didn't have to spell out what I meant by "or else." It meant the Big D, which did not stand for Dallas. "Or else" meant lawyers, misery, and Emilia divided.

To be honest, I had my doubts about seeing a marriage counselor, too. It felt like a last-ditch effort, like a portal through which you pass on the way out of marriage. Still, there was nothing else to be done.

The morning of the appointment, Jim and I drove to the medical center in silence and headed down an unfamiliar hallway to Mental Health. But the therapist didn't show up. "There must have been some mix-up," said the receptionist.

"What?" I exploded. I don't remember what I said to the woman behind the desk, and I'm sure I should be ashamed of myself. I ran out in tears. It felt like a terrible omen.

We got another referral, along with an apology from Mental Health, and a few weeks later Jim and I found ourselves sitting across from a tall, thin man with a long, thin nose. He asked me why I had gotten so upset about being stood up (the other counselor had had a family emergency). I told him that I'd been through this already. I'd been married before and had gone to counseling with my first husband just before we split up. I guess, deep down, I was expecting a repeat performance.

The therapist pointed out that this was a whole new ball game with new players. He also said that, my previous experience notwithstanding, marriage counseling usually works.

We saw him six times. Jim talked about how hard it had been to lose three jobs in the space of a year. Working for elected officials is notoriously volatile, but it doesn't make getting laid off feel any less personal. And becoming a dad had made Jim vulnerable in new ways; he was afraid of failing as a father, husband, and provider.

I laid out my fears of being swallowed by domesticity. My writing career was on hold and I was starting to wonder if I'd ever be able to string two coherent sentences together again. Although I was happy and a little surprised to discover how competent I felt in my role as a mother, I also felt trapped by the minutiae of being primary parent, housekeeper, and cook. There were days I wanted to scream, "Where's the rest of me?"

Maybe we had said some of these things to each other at home, but we certainly hadn't heard as much as we did with a trained third party in the room. I'm not sure which was more important, the counselor's well-crafted questions or simply the example of his undivided attention, but soon, Jim and I began to untangle the past from the present and to loosen fears from facts.

Jim was not just like his father, who had abandoned his family after years of estrangement. And all my emotional eggs were not in the mommy basket. As much as I loved my new role, thirty-five years of opinioned womanhood were not going to evaporate in the warm glow of motherhood.

By way of "homework" the therapist suggested several

commonsense gimmicks. We were to spend ten minutes each evening debriefing about our respective days. We were to take turns and not interrupt each other. He also suggested regular sex dates. Sounds mechanical, but it sure takes the pressure off the rest of the week. And for heaven's sake, said the therapist, if you're fighting about who cleans the bathroom, why not just pay someone else to do it for you?

Jim and I couldn't afford a cleaning service, but otherwise we followed his advice, which did us good. The ice between us began to melt. We had uncorked the fear and worry. We could relax, which made us aware of the tension we'd been carrying. We went out for dinner.

In therapy, Jim and I found out that our laundry wasn't dirty so much as stale and in need of a good airing. We made our best confessions outside of the therapist's office, in restaurants—usually over dessert. He was terrified of messing up our daughter. I was terrified we'd never talk about anything or anyone else but our daughter. We needed more reassurance from each other about everything. We needed more sleep.

Once we spilled them, our secret worries began to look like the hill of beans they were. Our woes were manageable, some even laughable. Sleep? Hah!

On our way to the first therapy appointment, Jim and I had walked down the hallway in single file. Actually, I think I strode ahead of him in a self-righteous snit. An hour later, we walked out, side by side. We left our last session hand in hand, mostly reassured but also nervous, unsure of how we would maintain our fragile, new equilibrium. But the therapist had said we could always come back for a tune-up, and it's helpful to know that the offer still stands, a backstop, a comfort, our own private safety net.

BEDTIME STORY

AS A TEN-YEAR-OLD, Emilia declared, "It's not fair that you and Daddy get to sleep together and I'm all alone."

Already nearly five feet tall, my daughter had long ago outgrown the option of joining us in bed for anything but a quick hug. But I did feel sorry for the kid. As the glorious New England autumn takes its bitter turn, not even a stack of extra blankets can banish the chill on the first cold nights if you have to sleep by yourself.

In these latitudes, you walk around for four months with your shoulders hunched up around your ears. So snuggling beside the blast furnace of Jim's body is how I survive nor'easters, wind chills, and weeks when the sun doesn't shine.

Sharing a bed is one of the great delights of marriage, and not merely in the carnal sense. Bedded time is when couples touch and whisper and bask in unspoken and dependable tenderness and reassurance. Only babies are better cradled than a pair trading spoons: one body draping around the well-known back, and then switching places in unconscious exchange to nestle inside the intimate bowl between chest and knees.

The bedstead was our first major furniture purchase. We opted for a platform for the firmness and chose a double rather than queen- or king-size, because (a) a double bed would fit through the door, (b) it was cheaper, and (c) I had this naive theory that if our bed was small we would never go to sleep angry at each other. How could we possibly stay mad if we were touching?

Of course, on the steamy summer nights when even the spaces between my toes are sweating and Jim's arm feels like a hot stove, I curse our youthful stupidity. But as soon as the trees start to change color, I'm glad we went small. Besides, even if we shared a sultan-size mattress, our bed would still not be free of strife; it's not the snoring so much as the moaning.

Every few months, and for no apparent reason, Jim will suddenly, and almost every night, let out a groan so loud and sustained that our dog jumps off the bed and runs downstairs.

"Jim?" I say, wakened from a sound sleep and poking him just a little harder than I need to.

"Snergeraf?" he mumbles.

"You're moaning."

"Sorry," he says, pats me on the back, and rolls over. Three, six, or nine minutes later, just as I'm nodding off, he lets out another heartrending groan. This time, he wakes himself up. "Sorry."

"Harrumph," I reply, unappeased, and in the morning recount the downside of sharing a bed to Emilia.

But just when I'm starting to worry about ever getting a full night's sleep again, the moaning mysteriously ceases. I give silent thanks to the sandman, hug Jim extra tight, and smugly listen to the north wind rattle the windows. I don't tell Emilia that. It would be gloating. But I do hope that she will eventually discover what she's been missing when she'd old enough to share a bed with someone as nice as her dad.

FIREFLIES

MY HUSBAND AND I celebrated our tenth anniversary very quietly. Actually, "celebrate" is probably too strong a word. Since the date coincided with Emilia's dance recital, we dispensed with the candlelit dinner for two. There was certainly no diamond anniversary band—not after putting a new roof on the garage.

It's not that we ignored the occasion altogether. Jim encouraged me to get the bracelet I was hankering after, and I bought him a lesson with a golf pro. That was pretty much it.

I'm not complaining. I love my husband and my husband loves me and after a decade that seems a triumph in itself.

Nevertheless, it's clear that I'm not talking about the kind of love swamping the radio dial. In popular songs, it is romance that reigns, always new and breathless and reminding me of the passion that lofted Jim and me into the stratosphere, and thence into marriage.

I have a box of poems as proof of our residence in that rarefied air. But they are souvenirs. There is no way to recapture that time—no matter where we go on vacation or how flimsy my nightgown. Romantic love is precious and wild precisely because it cannot be bottled.

There is only the present, in which love is more down-to-earth though still, occasionally, magical. Romantic love is to married love as fireworks are to fireflies. Different as motorcycles and minivans, champagne and beer, and yet, both light up the night and gladden the heart.

Romance is the Fourth of July: explosions, ooh's and aah's, bright colors, and heavy breathing. The face of your beloved fills your consciousness like a sky replete with Roman candles. It's the greatest show on earth and the finale leaves you thrilled, exhausted, ears ringing.

The fireflies of married love punctuate the dark with silent lights. Their split-second beacons are always a golden surprise and proof that fairies do exist. You whisper in their presence and smile. You stare and try not to blink so as not to miss any. You call the kids to the porch to come look, too.

Fireflies disappear into the woods long before you're ready for them to go, or else the mosquitoes chase you back inside the house. But even when you can't see them, they're out there, flashing their insect Morse code of love. And they'll be there tomorrow night, and next summer, too, if you go look for them.

That's one of the secrets of married love—effort. Sometimes, it takes an enormous act of faith to overcome the inertia that pins you to the couch and go look for fireflies.

"Married love is not an emotion but a behavior," says a friend, quoting her therapist. In other words, if you sit around waiting to be swept away by warm feelings for your spouse, you're apt to get cranky and start pouting like a kid who didn't get the toy she saw advertised on television. But if you act lovingly, you're likely to generate hugs, back rubs, and the occasional floral bouquets in return.

I have a marriage mantra, too: "You only love them every other day."

I discovered this scrap of wisdom from "Arlo and Janis," a comic strip that chronicles the domestic ups and downs of a long-married couple with a growing son. Janis made this observation to a girlfriend over a glass of white wine. I say it to myself whenever fireflies are out of season.

"You only love them every other day" reminds me that, no matter how angry or disappointed or (dare I say it?) bored I am by my marriage, those feelings will eventually give way to joy, satisfaction, and, occasionally, fascination. I just wish that the formula really worked on an alternating-day basis; sometimes the "every other" applies to weeks and even months.

Autumn often musters in a dark season for Jim and me. After a summer of long sunsets and regular lightning-bug sightings, we get swallowed up by the September welter of work, school, holidays, head colds, heating bills. Then all of a sudden it's November, and we haven't seen a movie together since July.

I know that we'll climb out of our rut eventually. Sometimes, all we need is a night out in nice clothes to wake up the nerve endings that connect us to each other. Other times, it's a day of apple picking with our daughter.

It's not easy being married with children. Generally, the kids' needs come first, which is as it should be. Which is also why it's hard to go hunting for fireflies when the baby is teething.

I think childless couples have an easier time keeping the flame burning bright because they simply have more energy to devote to one another. Among child-free friends, I see more mutual tenderness, attentiveness, and politeness. He brings coffee to her in bed. She never shops without hunting for his favorite shirts. Their vacations look like a reprise of some European honeymoon I never had.

Of course, long-term child-free relationships are not all sizzle and spark. Those pairs bicker and some divorce never having known the intense, giddy infatuation of falling in love with your baby, or sharing sentimental tears beside a sleeping child's bed, or facing the awesome fact that someone needs you to love each other just as much as you love her.

Nobody told me any of this stuff. Despite the endless political posturing about the importance of marriage and family values, everything around us venerates romantic love, which is self-centered and deliciously antisocial.

Married love happens off-camera, long after the credits stop rolling. Novels about marriage tend to focus on discord, disintegration, and divorce. On television, it's either sitcom spouses trading zingers or widowers with pluck. To find a celebration of married love, you have to read the funny papers or the poetry of William Carlos Williams.

When I was in college, my favorite English professor, Harry Marten, taught a Williams poem he thought only married people could fully understand. He suggested reading it as though it were a note taped to the refrigerator door, intended for the one person in the world who would see its tenderness peeking through an almost careless apology.

THIS IS JUST TO SAY

*I have eaten
the plums
that were in
the icebox*

*and which
you were probably
saving*

for breakfast
Forgive me
they were delicious
so sweet
and so cold

Married love is in the details—the purloined plums, the casual kiss on the way out the door, the midday phone call just to say hi, the arm wrapped around your shoulders through a winter's night. It's not exactly happily ever after, but it's the only place I know to find fireflies in March.

MY ONE
AND ONLY

WHEN Emilia came along, everything changed. Which is why people have children, and why I had to write about her.

Parenthood is an adventure and an education. Our children show us countless miracles daily: they walk, they talk, they become capable of humor and compassion. And they leave us a little more every day.

But I didn't write about motherhood in the abstract. I wrote about being Emilia's mother. I was honest. I also tried to respect her privacy. And as soon as she could read, she had a veto.

She has two inches on me now. She is funny and brave and she sends her own regards. I have no doubt you'll be hearing from her someday, and sooner rather than later.

ONE

"DO YOU HAVE CHILDREN?"

It may be the simplest of all conversation openers, but it's a tricky question for me. I can't answer it with a simple "Yes," because I do not have "children."

"I have one," I say, and wait for the other shoe to drop.

"Only one?"

When I'm feeling spunky, I reply, "I stopped at perfection."

Family size is one of those topics that ought to be crossed off the list of things you discuss with strangers. There is too much pain attached to this area of life—too much infertility, too many miscarriages—to talk about it as though the subject were as neutral as the weather. I have several friends who had no choice but to stop after one, and for them the questions hurt.

For me, it was a choice. My husband and I agreed that three is cozy and complete. My daughter has asked, from time to time, why she has no brother or sister, and I have answered with the line (attributed to Brooke Astor's mother) about stopping at perfection. Emilia likes to hear that. Who wouldn't?

I also told her that I think our family is wonderful the way it is. As a six-year-old, she agreed, gave me a hug, and returned to her friends, her books, the dog.

I don't think being an only child caused her any suffering. Like most onlys, she thrived, excelled in verbal skills and charming adults, but is otherwise virtually indistinguishable from children who have siblings.

It's good for me, too. I love my work, I see my friends, and I've been able to give my daughter my undivided attention. My store of patience, such as it is, is at her disposal. I know I'm being the best mommy I can be and I'm quite sure I wouldn't be able to say that if we'd more than one.

Life with one child is simpler and easier. It is also less stressful economically. I don't mean to be crass; we never made a choice between a second baby and a Ferrari, but there was no family trust fund to cover Emilia's or any subsequent offspring's college tuition.

And yet, if one child is cheaper, the experience is more dear. We have only one shot at doing right by her, no second chance to learn all the lessons a child can teach. Parents with more than one confess that the second or third time they go to a "first" dance recital or Cub Scout open house, they have to dredge up the enthusiasm that came automatically with the oldest. For me, everything is not only a first but also a one-time-only opportunity, so I stay tuned; I knew it was the only kindergarten harvest festival I would ever attend and I cherished every chaotic moment. The only bat mitzvah. The only high school graduation.

As happy as I am with my choice, I do not proselytize the benefits of the one-child family. I rejoice with my friends over their seconds and thirds. I understand the desire for a larger family, and there are times when I envy the sweetness of a newborn's cooing, the moment that an older child takes her baby brother's hand to cross the street. Of course, my friends with two or three tell me how lucky I am to be free of the bickering that accompanies these joys. Every choice is a trade-off.

When my daughter was born, people asked me, "How do you like being a mother?" There was only one way I could answer: "I like being Emilia's mother." Had she been a colicky baby, my experience of new motherhood would not have been so satisfying. If she had been a less communicative and affectionate toddler, I might have felt the need for another child to fill my lap. If she had been a boy, I might have attempted another, since Jim and I had our hearts set on a daughter. But we got Emilia, who is more than we ever hoped for.

The size of my family is not the outcome of a single choice; it reflects countless details and decisions of my life story, and Jim's. It probably has something to do with the fact that my husband and I are both first children. I sometimes think that if I had been twenty-five instead of thirty-five at the birth of my first child . . . but that is a peculiar game. If I had been born in London instead of Brooklyn . . . If I could play the piano . . . If I were a carpenter . . .

In any of those cases, I wouldn't be me. I wouldn't have lived the life that has given me this terrific kid, who is neither lonely nor spoiled. Emilia is, however, completely sure of that place at the center of my heart. When I tell her that I love her, she smiles, shakes her head, and says, "Oh Mom, I know that."

Nursing a Dream

WHEN I DRIVE PAST the hospital where my daughter was born, I look up to the eleventh floor and wonder if the new moms up there are doing what I did when I was in their johnnies: I was hoping that my baby would grow up to be a nurse. Actually, hoping is kind of a wishy-washy word for it. I was so grateful for the ministrations and support of the labor and delivery nurses, I more or less pledged my newborn's life as a thanks offering to Florence Nightingale.

This is a terribly unfashionable wish. Nobody surprises a two-year-old with a nurse's kit. I don't think they even make those anymore. Hoping that your kid studies hard, gets into a good college, and becomes a nurse is something like hoping that he or she studies hard, goes to Harvard, and becomes vice president.

We are supposed to want our children to become physicians. We are pointedly supposed to want *daughters* to become doctors. Life insurance companies seem particularly smitten with this idea; the advertising image of Mommy and Daddy musing about a medical school graduation over pink bunting is pop-culture shorthand for the death of sexist stereotypes.

Not that I have anything against the profession that seeks to cure. I'm sure that I would be every inch the parodied proud Jewish mother if she should go to medical school.

But I have a different fantasy. Emilia applies to both the best medical schools and the finest nursing programs in the country. She is accepted by them all, of course. And she chooses to become a nurse.

In the best of all possible futures, this decision would not cost her a penny of earning potential, not one iota of status, not a smidgen of respect. I have hope for the twenty-first century, but I'm not banking on that kind of revolution. I know it would cost her dearly to choose the path of the ill-paid angels instead of the route of the medical deities.

What kind of a mother wishes upon her daughter a life of awful hours, terrible smells, and three-dimensional exhaustion for which she will be paid less than a garbage collector earns? Why do I want her on the front lines of human life, staring down death and despair during twelve-hour shifts, while the glory goes to some first-year resident who knows less than she does?

But really, I am no different from every other parent who wishes her child a better life than her own, though that wish is almost always understood in financial terms. I have, of course, entertained the thought of an opulent retirement at my offspring's expense, but I have to confess that I'm not set on her becoming a member of the plumbers' union.

What kind of emotional satisfaction would she feel after a day of cleaning clogged drains? For that matter, what kind of happiness comes of spending a seventy-hour workweek fast-tracking to the top of a heap of money?

I want her to do better than her father and me in so many ways. She should be more athletic than we two slugs. She should know the names of all the wildflowers. She should eat more fish and enjoy mathematics. But my dearest ambition is that she surpass us in the empathy department. Not the reading-about-sad-stuff-and-being-moved kind of empathy, but the working-to-make-a-difference kind.

I told a friend about the unfashionable ambition I harbor for my daughter. But after I explained, he said it's not the job that matters and that I would probably be just as proud if she were a banker who helped low-income people get mortgages.

In theory he's right. Besides, I have seen awful nurses—cold, aloof, and too busy to smile at a terrified old man.

There are nurse majordomos and nincompoop nurses. The diploma does not automatically bestow a kind heart, and neither does internal plumbing. The least sympathetic doctor I ever had was a woman.

I knew from age ten that my daughter would not be an Olympic gymnast, or thrill to the mysteries of calculus. She will go her own way no matter what I wish for her.

Nursing—97 percent female, underpaid, and under-valued—is the only profession whose official mandate is comfort. No matter what she does with her life, I want my kid to know that there is no higher calling.

TENDER TRIANGLE

WHEN EMILIA WAS a little girl, I was involved in a series of love triangles—complicated, three-sided relationships, sometimes acute, sometimes obtuse, but always drawn with self-doubt, longing, jealousy, and shifting loyalties.

I am not talking about the lurid geometry of three people who, sharing adult and carnal feelings, are joined in a polygon of passion, danger, and pain. I do not refer to the eternal mess of Arthur, Lancelot, and Guinevere, or to the situation, equally archetypal, that still festers among Archie, Reggie, and Veronica. I am not that kind of girl.

I was, however, a mother with a child in day care. And from her third month to her fifth year, I found myself triangulated, inhabiting one corner of a three-way relationship of which I had no inkling, and for which there was no preparation. The child-rearing books did not provide a clue.

The books and articles tell you to shop for day care more or less the way you would select an attorney. They advise you to make checklists and arrange visits. Investigate credentials. Obtain references. Weigh the pros and cons. They never say anything about making a leap of faith. They say nothing about anybody falling in love.

Which is really what's at stake. The day care center's license may be in order, sugary snacks and war toys forbidden. But if the baby-sitter and the baby who spend hours and days together do not love each other, it will not do. The infant will not smile in the mornings. The parents will snap at each other. The au pair will be sick more and more often.

The odd thing is, when they do love—with all the private jokes and ways of doing and knowing that love comprises—a triangle is formed, charged and awkward. Two adults (or three or four, depending), who might have been as different from and indifferent to each other as horses and camels, now share something as intimate as diapers. Your darling's eyes light up at the sight of the not-mother who is like-mother. His arms reach up to her for lunch, for comfort. How wonderful. How wrenching.

Parent and teacher, mother and sitter, father and nanny, we are connected to each other through the love of the same child. But this feels weird; after all, it's a cash transaction and paying for love can be nothing but tawdry.

It is also embarrassing because there's not enough money in the world to pay for the time my daughter's baby-sitter enjoyed and cared for her while I filled pages with words. And yet, the money I paid was horribly inadequate. The dog catcher made more.

Congenitally rich people have much more experience with this three-sided configuration. Nobility and old money have always entrusted children, from infancy onward, to nannies and then boarding schools. I used to think of nursemaids and nannies in precisely the same way I did as a child: as jailers or as Mary Poppins. But now I am intrigued by the uneasy truce between Mary Poppins (a good witch disguised as a nanny) and the terminally stiff-upper-lipped father of her young charges.

It certainly never occurred to Mr. Banks to examine his relationship to the woman who was giving his children those breathless lessons in manners and imagination. Then again, the British are famous for the way they maintain a formal distance between upstairs and downstairs, separating love from even the most tender service.

Americans are not used to that kind of artifice. We know our nannies to be our equals. We recognize love when we see it. And it makes for a lot of newfangled triangles.

However, this sort of intimacy is usually acknowledged only in its breach, like when suspicious parents hide a video camera and catch the baby-sitter in the act of slapping the baby. The day after one of those stories aired on the evening news, I went to retrieve Emilia from the sitter, who was almost purple with outrage. Our heads shook in shared disgust, but I'm quite sure we did not make eye contact. It was as though the wretch who smacked the baby (again, and again, and again, in the television replays) had compromised our covenant.

But that was not possible. Barbara loved Emilia and Emilia loved Barbara. And I counted us lucky, times three.

ARTFUL

"EVERYONE IN MY school is an artist," said Emilia as we walked home one afternoon.

The cluttered walls of preschools and the neat bulletin boards in elementary schools testify to the accuracy of her opinion. All children, given half a chance, are artists. They come running up to Mom or Pop, or the grandparents, or any agreeable adult, waving a sheet of paper thick with poster paint or barely scratched by a pencil, with the same triumphant demand: Look at what I made!

Maybe I cannot tie my shoes or control what time I have to go to bed, but I made this blob, this line, this face with the corkscrew hair and the emphatic ears. Look at this proof of the wonderfulness of me: I can make a hat, a rocket, a flower, a turtle, where before there was nothing. Look. Tell me how great it is. Tell me how great I am.

Whatever it looks like, it is priceless.

I could never draw as well as my daughter. Sure, it was easier to tell the difference between my dogs and spiders, but her critters were so lively that they made the page wiggle, whereas mine just sort of lay there, splayed and fake. Sitting beside her at the kitchen table, brushes in our hands and sheets of construction paper before us, I hesitated and fretted. She would just get down to work, making gifts for her grown-up friends. "This one is for Sandy," she said. "This one is for Margaret."

Most adults are pretty bad at art. We stop making it when we learn the rules about talent and criticism and competition. We stop looking at it, as children do, for fun.

When my daughter brought home her pictures and collages and clay dragons, it was clear to me that art is hardwired, like language. Once in a while, I remember that for myself. At a museum, I laugh at a landscape, or itch to touch a sculpted shoulder, or peer inside a one-of-a-kind cupboard, and I'm challenged and comforted by the handmade-ness, by the mind and fingers behind the beauty. Those experiences of art are kinetic and connected to the "Look at what I made" still in the process of happening.

My favorite pieces from Emilia's oeuvre still hang in the house. I had to toss most of it, just to keep from drowning in paper, and I remember feeling a guilty twinge as I consigned each developmental stage to oblivion. Usually, I waited until she slept to make room on the fridge for her latest triumphs. She didn't notice when her old things vanished in the night; there was always more where that came from. Besides, the particular picture wasn't the issue. For her, "art," like "eat," was a verb, a daily requirement and a dependable pleasure.

READING MATERIAL

IT WAS BIG NEWS at my house the day Emilia read her first book.

We'd gone to the library with a list provided by her kindergarten teacher, but most of those titles were out. So the librarian helped us find others, including *The Yellow Boat* by Margaret Hillert.

"Look here, look here.

"See the little boat.

"See the yellow boat."

She read the whole thing—all twenty-seven pages, all forty-three words—while sitting on my lap as we rode the train downtown to have a ladies' lunch and see the cat show. All in all, it was a big day. So big, in fact, that I recorded it in her baby book, in which the last entry related to events in the bathroom.

Reading a book did not make my daughter a kindergarten prodigy. Anthony, a fellow pupil, was far and away the best reader in her class. This was evident at the Thanksgiving assembly, when Anthony stood up before a packed auditorium and read a few paragraphs loaded with sixth-grade words.

They did not teach reading, per se, in my daughter's kindergarten, but the room was full of words and letters. It was part of the "whole language" approach, which involved steeping the kids in an alphabet-soup kind of atmosphere until they absorbed some of the flavor, without even trying. It's not really learning by osmosis; all sorts of cognitive processes are going on inside those young heads. But it seems virtually effortless in comparison with adult language acquisition. The very idea of mastering a new alphabet makes my limbs feel heavy and my brain ache.

Of course, my daughter was in training for that milestone since birth. Jim and I read to her every day since infancy. And as a longtime resident of *Sesame Street*, where words are sold as cleverly as soap is on the networks, she was a savvy consumer of letters, numbers, colors, geometric shapes, and literacy itself.

Put it together and what have you got? *The Yellow Boat* and then *Horton Hears a Who*, followed by the Ramona books and *The Secret Garden*. After that, it's just a hop, skip, and a jump to *Great Expectations*.

I remember learning to read in first grade with Dick and Jane, Spot and Puff, and Mother, who always wore an apron over her shirtwaist dress. I remember letters arranged around the top of the blackboard and how they shifted into focus. One day it was gibberish, the next day I saw words that were as familiar as my own mother's face: "that," "in," "this," "on," "after."

All in all, Emilia was pretty blasé about starting to read. When grown-ups asked her, "What's new?" she couldn't think of an answer. Not me. I remember running into the living room to announce to my husband that she'd just read the words "join the fun" on a birthday party invitation. It was "join" that impressed me.

I was a bit more cautious about sharing this news outside my immediate family. I was proud but I didn't really want to boast, though it's kind of hard to avoid. We parents are a fierce tribe, defensive of our young and quick to take offense. There's comfort and support in comparing notes about first teeth and worst tantrums. But there is also, I fear, competition.

Parents make comparisons and then feel sheepish or guilty when we judge our own offspring as anything less than the best. I must confess to envying the reflected glory that shone upon Anthony's mom while he read all those polysyllabic words for the whole school.

I noticed, however, that parents of older children welcomed my news without a lick of defensiveness, offering me big welcome-to-yet-another-club smiles. "Isn't it exciting?" they said, proceeding to the story of their children's first book report. It's always the same amazing, cherished story. It was just my turn to tell it.

"Go, yellow boat, go."

LEARNING TO LET GO

"BYE, MOM," SHE SAID, and off she went. Seven years old and walking to school all by herself.

I lifted the curtain on the front door and watched her stroll down the street, her red-yellow-blue backpack bouncing to every step. She turned the corner and disappeared into her very own day. She did not look back.

Something had ended. Something else had begun.

I called my husband and told him the news. At work, I announced it to anyone who said so much as "good morning" to me. Parents of children younger than mine looked slightly stricken at the prospect of so momentous a step into the great unknown. They asked, only half joking, if I had followed her in the car, wearing dark glasses and a fake nose.

But I had not, and I even resisted the temptation of calling the school to make sure she had arrived safely. I knew she was okay. After all, it is only six blocks from our house. The school crossing guard at the busy intersection, a grandmotherly type, knew my daughter's name. If she'd gone missing or been hit by a car, someone would have called me.

Which is not to say that I put the whole matter out of my head and got on with the rest of my busy day. In my mind's eye, I did follow her around the first corner and across the quiet side streets on the route we had practiced together many times.

I pictured her kicking through the piles of leaves on Cherry Street, feeling big and strong, knowing the crunching music was all her own doing. I imagined her thinking about the day ahead—gym in the afternoon, but first, the spelling test: "Learning." "Necessary." "Endure."

She was following in my footsteps—on a route I traveled years ago and miles away—through the leaves to Maple Avenue School and a crossing guard named Lee, in a blue uniform and police hat, who said hello to me every morning.

The same day my daughter walked to school by herself for the first time, a friend, who is only five years my senior, put her daughter, also my friend, on an airplane for a trip around the world. After a stop in London, the twenty-one-year-old was off to Cairo, Bombay, Singapore, and Jakarta. Her itinerary hung on my refrigerator door, right next to the week's spelling list: "Misbehave." "Remember." "Enjoy." She got my letter in Bangkok.

I do not usually get sentimental about my daughter's milestones. I did not get teary when my daughter started kindergarten, lost her first tooth, or stopped asking me to kiss her boo-boos. But something about her walking out the door alone made me feel left behind.

"Oh, Mom," she said, rolling her eyes, as I reported the news to her grandparents on the telephone. "It's no big deal." The next day, though, as she put on her coat to leave for school, she invited me, rather shyly, to come along.

We crunched through the last of the leaves together, and she practiced her spelling words out loud: "Different." "Harvest." "Celebrating."

BEACH BEACON

MY BEACH UMBRELLA is striped, red and white. It was a wedding gift, something we put on the bridal registry but were still surprised to find amid the serving platters and mixing bowls.

Turns out, it was one of the most useful things we got. A sturdy contraption, with a white-enameled pole and heavy cotton-duck cover, the umbrella was our landmark for ten summers. Like our own North Star, or territorial flag, it pointed the way back to blanket and family after a walk to the far end of a crowded beach.

Not everyone lugs an umbrella to the beach. It's a pain to carry, not to mention a poke-in-the-eye waiting to happen. But if there's a baby in your party, or if too much sun makes you dizzy, as it does me, you've got to haul one.

As much as I need and like my umbrella, though, I know it marks me as something of a geezer. There's no use denying it with self-righteous speeches about the ravages of skin cancer.

I see the slim girls who carry nothing but a towel, a bottle of tanning oil, and a can of diet cola. They peel off their shorts and absorb the heat of the day with mystic concentration. Sun worshiping may be officially out of fashion, but the cult still thrives, because when you lie prone or supine, motionless and baking, it feels like the sun is worshiping you. Which is as close as you can get to the physical sensation of immortality here on earth.

The girls on the towels seem oblivious to the social landscape of the beach: old people sitting on lawn chairs from their backyards, honeymoon couples reading novels in sleek new sand chairs, crying babies, children attached by string to kites shuddering on high.

Sun-stunned, the girls remain unmoved by the living beer commercial that unfolds nearby: strapping volleyball boys who cheer every spike and point. No umbrella for them either, just a cooler the size of Texas.

It's never too early or too late to drink and eat at the beach. Suds, soda, sandwiches, fruit, cookies, crackers, cheese, popcorn. Children, perpetually hungry, track sand all over the blanket, looking for something else. There are never enough potato chips.

I envy the people who dish out fried chicken and potato salad on sturdy paper plates, who pull home-baked cookies out of their hampers and have bottomless plastic containers full of chilled grapes, and who never run out of lemonade. They make me, with my carrot sticks and pretzels, feel deprived and deserving of chocolate ice cream—which tastes better when your lips are salty from the sea.

My daughter was partial to chocolate-chip-cookie-dough ice cream, which she earned by putting in a full day's work: swimming, digging, hunting for shells, rocks, crabs. She judged the waves (that was a good one, that one didn't crash) and formed instant friendships that dissolved like sugar when it was time to go. She came back to our umbrella to ask for a cookie, or to ask why we weren't in the water or playing Frisbee or applauding her every dive and somersault. She could barely keep from asking, "What's wrong with you, anyway?"

I remember my parents sitting in lawn chairs under a tree by the lake, talking with their friends, wasting whole afternoons. I took it as a personal victory when my father would finally relent and come into the water, which he claimed to love. But after only a few minutes, he'd be drying himself off, telling me to go and play with my brother. He was like the rest of the grown-ups, after all.

And now, of course, so am I. With family and friends, under the striped red-and-white umbrella, planted, and for the moment as happy as a clam.

DEAR EMILIA

HAPPY BIRTHDAY. This week you turn thirteen. You are now bat mitzvah.

I know, I know. Synagogue schedules being what they are, you won't be reading from the Torah and we won't be dancing the hora for several more weeks, but as of November 4, the mitzvot are yours. More to the point, you belong to them.

My friend, Rabbi Liza Stern, told me that when her children reached the age of thirteen, she realized that they were no longer son and daughter of Liza and Keith only; they were also son and daughter of the mitzvah.

You know that mitzvah means commandment, but it

also means community and commitment. It's my job to give you up, not only to your raging individuality, but also to your rightful place at the table. You have come to show us something altogether new, to shake things up, to teach us your Torah.

Actually, this happens to all kids around your age, whether or not a kid has a bar or bat mitzvah, whether or not a kid is even Jewish. It just happens. You age into it. But it's such a powerful process, I'm glad for the ritual that makes us stop and acknowledge what's going on.

We are all turning thirteen this week. Daddy and I have been parents for thirteen years. A few months ago, when I closed my eyes to light candles on Friday night, I was startled to realize that your voice no longer rose up from somewhere below my ear. You are as tall as I am. You grow more beautiful by the week (you don't have to take my word for this; I can supply affidavits).

I know we argue a lot. I try to remember that arguing, even door slamming, is what thirteen-year-olds do. I try to remember that there can be no bat mitzvah without arguing. It's part of the life cycle, part of making your own thirteen-year-old way, part of my letting go of the little kid who sat on my lap and held my earlobe like a talisman.

So even though you will not chant Torah and haftarah for a few weeks yet, this week you become bat mitzvah, and in honor of the occasion, Daddy and I will give you a new blessing this Shabbat.

Up until now, we used the traditional formula: *Y'sim-*

eych Elohim, k'Sara, Rivka, Rachel, v'Leah. May God make you as Sarah, Rebecca, Rachel, and Leah.

I was never entirely comfortable with that prayer, and once you grew old enough to understand it, you didn't like it much either. It was strange to pray for you to be like anyone else—even those four remarkable women. I have never wanted you to be anyone but who you are.

You know the stories of Sarah, Rebecca, Rachel, and Leah, and I think you consider them your metaphorical foremothers. But now, as you take on the mitzvah of becoming your own woman, it is time for a change.

So here is a new prayer for you. It comes from *The Book of Blessings* by the poet and liturgist Marcia Falk.

Esther Leah, *Hayi asher tihyi.*

Emilia, who is also sometimes known as Mimi, Be who you are. And may you be blessed in all that you are.

THE MOTHER'S
BAT MITZVAH SPEECH

A FEW MONTHS AGO, when Daddy and I offered to give you the tallit you are wearing today for your own, I don't think you realized how happy you made us.

I know there are other prayer shawls that have more appeal for a thirteen-year-old girl, especially the beautiful multicolored silk ones. I think you've even had second thoughts since you said yes to taking this one. But I hope that, in the long run, you'll be glad you did.

By accepting this tallit, you've created an heirloom. A few months before Daddy and I got married, I decided to give him a prayer shawl as a wedding gift, which could serve as our *huppah* and represent our Jewish home together.

In the pages of *The Jewish Catalog,* which was a kind of 1970s crunchy granola Whole Earth encyclopedia and Yellow Pages, I found the name and address of a Protestant minister who, in his retirement, had taken up the interesting hobby of weaving prayer shawls. Which is how it came to pass that the Reverend W. Sydney Fisher of Bethlehem, Pennsylvania, made this tallit, in shades of blue that include the exact color of your eyes.

Daddy tied the first set of fringes on this tallit in the days before our wedding, with the help of our friend Alan Pullman, who is here today. It was lifted over our heads in this room when we got married. And another friend Sondra Stein, who dressed the Torah for you today, held up one of the corners of the *huppah.*

A few years after our wedding, Daddy and I carried you up to this *bimah* (altar). You were a tiny bundle wrapped in the tallit you wear so gracefully today. This is the spot where you were given the name by which you were called to the Torah: Esther Leah—a name that honors my grandmothers Esther Leah and Esther Malkah.

Lots of the people in this room today were here that day, too, including my father, your Opa, whose memory is a blessing. He would have been delighted by your *d'rash,* by your Hebrew chanting, by the person you're becoming—just as your two grandmothers are delighted and proud.

Over the years, you played with this tallit, sitting next

to Daddy and me at High Holiday services and Shabbat services, too. You played hide-and-seek underneath it; you braided and unbraided the fringes, as children do.

But today, Emilia, Mimi, Esther Leah, you're not a child and the tallit belongs to you. You have already made it your own. Your fringes include the mysterious blue thread, called *t'chalit*, which were sent by your friend Mark Feldman, a gift from Jerusalem. And with a little help from Rabbi Kushner, you tied these fringes yourself.

The knots symbolize your connection to the mitzvot, the commandments incumbent upon adult Jews. As of today, the mitzvot are yours to study and to wrestle with, and to keep.

Today, you accept the Torah for yourself wrapped in the family tallit that now belongs to you. How will you understand the Torah, Emilia, and how will you teach it? Where will you take this tallit and to whom, eventually, will *you* give it?

Daddy and I look forward to learning the next chapters in the story of this tallit as it accompanies you through the where and how and whom of your Jewish life.

Esther Leah: *Hayi asher tihyi.*

Emilia: Be who you are.

Vahayi bruchah ba'asher tihyi.

And may you be blessed in all that you are.

COLUMBINE

THE MASSACRE AT Columbine High School occurred six months before my daughter started high school, and she took to heart the frightening idea that something like that could happen anywhere. Personalizing the cliché given voice by so many commentators and public officials, Emilia said, "Newton, Massachusetts, is not so different from Littleton, Colorado."

My daughter was frightened on behalf of friends who were already attending our high school, and she was worried about her own safety, too. She thought that the teachers ought to devise an escape plan, just in case something awful happened. She could not tolerate the idea that it was

impossible to safeguard against the contingencies of mad-
men. She wanted a guarantee, and it was my job to tell her
that there are none.

In the copycat aftermath that swept the country, there
was an empty bomb threat at my daughter's high school.
There were swastikas in the bathroom, and hideous, threat-
ening letters. It was my job to tell her that most human
beings do the right thing most of the time. I said things like,
"If you don't believe in the basic decency of humanity, you
might as well not get out of bed in the morning."

But my daughter had been studying the Holocaust in
Hebrew school. Why should she listen to me?

I hated those two murderous boys in Littleton, Colorado. I hated their parents and their teachers, and the
principal and the probation officer. I hated the jocks and
the cheerleaders, the guidance counselors and the idiots
who bought guns and ammunition for seventeen-year-old
kids. I grieved for them, too, but how dare those adults not
see what was going on in their own houses? It poisoned the
air, half a continent away, in my house.

I waited for some story that would enable me to understand the cause, which would then permit me to set the
danger to one side. I wanted it to be the parents' fault. Not
very nice of me, but maybe that would explain something
at least. Listening to clips from the funerals on the radio
and reading the eulogies in the newspapers unsettled me
even more than the lack of explanations.

"She is with God."

"He is in a better place."

"I'll see you in heaven, darling."

This kind of consolation sounds strange in my Jewish ears. Although some Jews believe that there is life after death, our funerals offer no guarantees. Jewish eulogies remind us only of what has been lost and can never be replaced.

Of course, when a grandparent dies, full of years and mourned by his generations, we can number the memories and smile through tears. But when a child is taken, there is no minimizing the agony. We howl at the injustice and even hold God accountable. We accept the blow, because we have no other choice, but there is no silver lining in the loss.

The obituaries for the children of Littleton, Colorado, were obscenely brief. "He liked to play video games." "She had just gotten her driver's license." Those lives were unredeemed promises, gone to the grave.

The Littleton funerals frightened me no less than the shootings. Why safeguard this life if the afterlife is better? Why limit gun sales if heaven awaits the victims of cruelty, senseless violence, accidents, suicide? Why set up metal detectors?

Jews answer those questions with a commandment from the Bible: "Choose life." This life. Here on earth. Temporal and corporal, beautiful and holy, and when children pick up guns, agonizing and raw and wrong.

FRIDAY NIGHT AT THE CROSSROADS

EVER SINCE SHE was born, my daughter has spent Friday evenings—from Shabbat dinner to bedtime—with me and my husband. But things are different now. Emilia is five feet eight inches tall. She has places to go, people to see, and a driver's license. Her presence at Shabbat dinner is required and acceptable to her, though these days she'd just as soon dispense with the parental blessing.

But after the meal? Pul-eeze.

Can she go to Becca's house? Can Dan come over? There's a dance at school. There's a rehearsal for the play.

A bunch of kids are watching a movie at Maya's. Unless there are legitimate and compelling family reasons (guests for dinner, a special event at temple), after dinner, she may go. And go she does.

I knew this was coming. After her bat mitzvah, Jewish observance became more and more a matter of her own choosing. I can remind and I can nag, I can and do put my foot down when it's important enough. But ultimately she will choose for herself how to be Jewish.

This is one of the hardest parts of being a liberal Jew. I made a lot of choices about my own practice, and I believe in my right to make them. Now that my child is nearly grown, I have to respect and defend her decisions, too. I try to remember that her Jewish choices will change over time—mine certainly have.

If I sound like I'm talking myself into this, that's because I am. This isn't easy.

On the day Emilia walked to school by herself for the first time, my heart was in my mouth, but she knew how to cross streets safely and what to do if a stranger approached, so I let her go. She came home, safe and sound.

Day after day, my daughter enters a world I know less and less about. At this point in my parenting career, one of my most important and difficult jobs is to give her a safe space in which to practice making decisions. Our big parent-child arguments revolve around which decisions Jim and I are ready to let her make.

The childhood that deposits my kid on this teenage

shore was marked by Hebrew blessings, family time, synagogue time, Jewish summer camp, Hebrew school, holiday celebrations, life-cycle celebrations, youth group, and love.

I have my fingers crossed. More than that, I have faith.

THE GOOD SHIP

FAMILY relationships are sanctified and legalized and acknowledged in newspaper announcements. Friends are linked together by informal, secular bonds that inevitably get short shrift. Writing about the importance of my friends—new and old, female and male, human and canine—felt like a way of balancing the scale a little.

Friends are cast as the secondary players but, in fact, they are as essential as bread, as crucial as chocolate. Friends provide a kind of sustenance without which life isn't just poorer, it's impossible.

My supporting cast does just that—they hold me up. They also tell me when I'm full of baloney and when it's time to update my eye makeup. I know they'll show up when it matters, and with that kind of safety net, it's much easier to take a chance on life's next big thing.

We piece together bits of family lore, scraps from old love affairs, hints of sibling animosities—tidbits shaken loose during conversations about something else entirely.

When your children are young, it's especially hard to start the process. The frustration of *conversation interruptus* can unravel the thread of the most intimate exchange. Even if you're meeting in the relative peace of a kid-free workday lunch, the clock is always ticking.

It's an interesting locution—*making* friends. It reminds me of a greeting card with a lady in an apron whose bubble says, "For your birthday, I'm going to make you a cake. . . . Poof! You're a cake." As if you could just run up to a likely candidate and shout, "Abracadabra! You're a friend."

To make friends, you need to mosey, to digress. In fact, you need a minimum of twenty-four uninterrupted, non-working hours. That's how long it takes to tell someone where you come from, what TV shows you make a point of watching, and how you'd spend a million dollars. It's also important to share three meals and see each other's face by the light of morning, noon, and night.

I timed it. Valerie, a work acquaintance who lives in Manhattan, and I decided we wanted to become friends, so we booked a room in a country inn. I arrived around four; we started talking and didn't stop until long after the town's church clock filled our room with midnight bells.

The next morning we continued, comparing income, theology, cosmetics. We talked about our other friends and how we met our husbands. We admired each other's earrings. We compared photographs of our children. We talked about our travels and our health. We talked about the homeless and how we react when someone asks us for money on the street. We talked about living wills. We talked about movies and movie stars and mothers and sex. The experience was a little like going to summer camp, or a weekend at college. It was also a little sad, since we live miles apart. But our twenty-four hours sealed the deal between us.

Once you get past second grade, making friends requires a lot of effort. It's worth it. The process bears some comparison with falling in love: There has to be a kind of mutual attraction. A signal is passed—some shared hilarity or a sentence finished with precisely the same words—and suddenly the room seems brighter. Hey! We could change our lives forever. We could make ourselves into friends.

GIRLFRIENDS,
IN PARTICULAR

WOMEN'S FRIENDSHIPS ARE, I think, one of the great secrets of the social universe. When you see pairs of women, sometimes threesomes or foursomes, from the outside, it might seem they are "just" having lunch, or drinking coffee, or walking around the neighborhood, or even shopping. But all this activity is, in fact, the methodology of friendship, the ways women connect and keep each other sane. It goes on by phone and e-mail and Hallmark, too.

This is not trivial activity. From the outside, it might appear casual, but these relationships are, in fact, the bedrock of contentment. We witness and we cheer, we

101

commiserate and we prod. We lean on each other and we prop each other up. We tell each other the truth. We sustain one another.

My women friends—some of whom I've known for thirty years, some of whom I've known for three months—sustain me in ways I couldn't begin to enumerate. At least not publicly.

We all love our families, but the truth is, they drive us nuts. Without friends, a lot of us would run screaming out of our homes at all hours of the day and night, ready to hand our children over to passing motorists, to flee spouses who snore or are laundry-challenged, to avoid the well-meaning "corrections" of siblings and parents.

Our friends listen to us complain about our families. They validate and sympathize with the problems that are genuine, and help us see when we're overreacting. Friends don't nag. I think that may be the definition of a friend.

You can't pick your parents or your kids. Marriage, though not quite as irrevocable, suffers similar pitfalls of too much familiarity.

So what is it about friendship that avoids that kind of craziness? Maybe it's just the different perspective. Maybe it's the voluntary nature of friendship, which is so clearly a gift, bestowed. The time we share with friends is, almost by definition, time carved out of family obligations, work, housekeeping, reading, gardening, even sleep. We're grateful to each other for making this choice—this gift—of our time.

Friends meet each other's expectations on a need-to-speak basis. Friends will show up when it matters, and when it doesn't, we trust the foundation will remain firm.

Of course, not all friendships last forever. Friends move and the commitment fades. Friends marry badly, or change too much, though I am still friends with a high school pal who votes Republican.

When friends die, we are heartbroken and bereft. The world goes dark but the phone doesn't ring with condolence. No one gives us time off from work to grieve the loss of this particular, precious, mostly unspoken love.

WITH A FRIEND IN MOURNING

UNTHINKABLE NEWS, unspeakable sorrow. My friend's baby died.

Word spread quickly, and mutual acquaintances called to see if I'd spoken with her, and asked, "How is she doing?"

I stammered one of several answers: She is devastated. She's crying a lot. She and her husband are hanging on to each other for dear life. She's going to be okay. She will never be the same. She's doing as well as can be expected.

There was nothing false in any of these statements, and yet none of them rang true. Even when I rattled off the whole list, something essential was missing, something about the terrible wisdom now etched on her face, visible even in the moments when she smiled at one of the small, inevitable pleasures of being alive, regardless.

People told me, "I feel so helpless. I can't think of anything to do for her."

But that wasn't so. She told me how much it helped when anyone called or wrote, if only to say, "I'm so sorry." When death pulls at you with that kind of force, every gesture of connection to the living counts for a lot.

Weeks after the baby's death, people were still calling to ask how my friend was doing, but I finally figured out what to tell them. "She is in mourning," I said, though I'm not always sure they heard the preposition. The phrase is *in* mourning—indicating a location, which is at some distance from those of us who are not.

It's an important distinction, because mourning is a real place in time, the precise location where "the valley of the shadow" is not a metaphor but a parallel universe. "I had no idea there was so much sorrow in the world," said my friend, who felt herself embraced with special tenderness by longtime mourners—people whose feelings of loss have mellowed but are no less a fact of their being, like an amputation.

I spent some time with my friend in mourning, which was wherever we happened to be those first months: at a restaurant during the lunch rush, or wandering through a stationery store where she went for paper to write sad thank-you notes. A rack of baby congratulations cards seemed to mock her, and I wanted to throw my coat over it or create some diversion so she wouldn't have to see the rows of smiling infants. I did nothing of the kind because there was no way to protect her against grief.

We walked into a bakery, and I wondered whether I should buy cupcakes for my daughter, who was in school at that moment, among faces and walls I could picture and visit. My friend's daughter was nowhere she could imagine and I was ashamed of my good fortune. But she had no use for my guilt, so I asked for the cupcakes.

We talked about her daughter and about God. She broke down and cried. I held her hand and bit my tongue to keep from trying to cheer her up.

Instead, I offered words and gestures that I'd never used before. As she drove away from my house, I pressed my hands together near my heart, in the Buddhist salutation of recognition and compassion I learned in yoga. I repeated a phrase I learned from my Quaker cousin: "I'm holding you in the light."

It didn't seem like enough. But sometimes, the least you can do is also the most.

A FOUR-WAY DEBATE

"LET'S MAKE IT A FOURSOME."

It's a phrase I don't think I've ever heard spoken. I've certainly never said it. But there it is, stuck in my brain, alongside the old Anacin commercial with the pounding hammer. I'm sure I first heard it on a rerun of the original *I Love Lucy*, a show that was really all about one of the great eternal rectangles of all time: Lucy and Ricky and Ethel and Fred.

On their own, the manic redhead and her Cuban consort probably would have been canceled after a couple of shrieking seasons. Only the addition of another couple—with the confidences between the women, collusions between the men, and intercouple gossip—allowed all those years to roll along, the four of them side by side by side by side. Not even the addition of little Ricky rocked that four-square boat.

In reality, little Rickys tend to upend the balance of friendships, at least for the first eight or ten years. Unless you can work it out the old-fashioned way, like my parents did, for their Sunday-evening canasta get-togethers. While four kids huddled around the latest episode of *Bonanza,* my mother and father sat in the kitchen with Jules and Loretta, where they played cards, ate rich desserts, drank strong coffee, and filled the ashtrays. (Sounds like an evening in Death Valley, doesn't it?)

Foursomes like that are rare, and for good reason. The geometry between two couples is difficult to figure and tough to maintain. All four people have to like one another, and with a certain degree of parity. The minute anyone says, "Love her, hate him," the paradigm is doomed. Oh, there might be an occasional dinner together, but forget canasta parties or spur-of-the-moment outings.

For two couples to become a foursome, a total of at least six compatible relationships must function simultaneously. One misunderstanding, one offense taken, and suddenly somebody is busy. All the time.

Thankfully, it is no longer essential for couples to socialize as though they were joined at the hip. Two can go off to exploding-car-chase movies, leaving the other two to mulch the lilacs. The crack-of-dawn yard sale fanatic from one household and his/her counterpart from the other will thoughtfully allow their disinterested spouses to sleep in peace.

Nevertheless, there is something comforting about being able to hang out quadraphonically. It is, as the therapists and parking lot attendants say, validating.

Living à deux is no picnic. It's not so much that you run out of things to discuss as the awful rudeness. People who share their money and toothpaste don't say "please" and "thank you" every time. They sometimes even forget to say hello and good-bye.

Adding even one other person to the scene raises the politeness ante. With another couple, there's an extra bonus: you get to watch how other people negotiate, tease, flare up, and forgive. Who clears the table? Who changes the diapers?

You discover what it takes for people as nice and smart as them (they are *your* friends, after all) to live together. You compare. You contrast. If you're lucky, you learn something.

There is something close to sacred about the relationship of long-standing foursomes. They eat Thanksgiving dinner together. They vacation on the same island. Other friends are important, but the inner circle is closed because it is full.

Actually, I never much liked *I Love Lucy* and remember little about the plots, except for one episode when Lucy and Ricky were flirting with another, higher-class couple. Fred and Ethel, acting like a pair of wounded elephants, stampeded the other two back into line. Where they stayed. Until the real-life divorce intervened.

WIDENING
THE CIRCLE

I HAVE A FRIEND WHO is twenty years younger than I. I first met her when she was twelve years old and the precocious daughter of friends who are much closer to my own age. I watched the girl's metamorphosis from childhood through adolescence. She attended my wedding and saw me take on the mantle of motherhood. She's a mom herself now, and my teenage baby looks up to her as a model of hip adulthood.

During all these years, Noa and I have spent relatively few hours alone together, but we have stayed in touch, connected by our own private line, which is both parallel to and separate from the ones that bind me to her mother and father.

When she started college in Providence, I drove down from Boston for a visit. I sat in on her psychology class, and she showed me her dorm room, a medley of Laura Ashley fabrics and arty magazine ads. I was flattered that she didn't feel the need to make the bed in anticipation of my visit.

During that afternoon together, we talked about her classes, her plans for an interdisciplinary major, the emotional intensity of living with so many other people. We talked about my daughter and about her father and we even talked a little about the fact that we were talking.

I am inordinately proud of this ongoing and ever-changing friendship. Discussing her emerging career, swapping CDs and cultural references, cooing over her daughter, all make me feel less locked into my own head, and my own circle, which sometimes feels tight and closed.

I say hello to all sorts of people in the course of a month, but the folks I sit down and eat with fall almost uniformly within a range no wider than five years in either direction. Peers to the left of me, peers to the right.

It's a great group and we have a lot to discuss. After all, we are passing through the same doorways at more or less the same pace. We understand each other, we rarely disagree.

Sameness is much safer and far more reassuring than diversity, but too much of the same can be less than challenging. It can, in extreme cases, lead to things far worse than mere monotony; homogeneity can crystallize into distrust, or even harden into bigotry.

I think I'm poorer for the fact that I never break bread with chemists or mathematicians, farmers, electricians, or police officers. There are no surgeons in my private address book, or Hindus, or people who revert to Spanish when they count their change. Everyone is white. Nearly everyone is female.

In any other time, I doubt I would have been able to share secrets with a teenager who wasn't a blood relative. And I certainly would never have been permitted the occasional pleasure of unchaperoned extra-familial male companionship. I'm lucky to have landed in a century and setting that permits me the possibility of exploring the difference between nineteen and thirty-nine, between male and female. I have yet to negotiate the distance between white and black, East and West, arts and sciences. But those stretches remain on the itinerary, which remains open, in anticipation of unforeseen destinations.

TO SIR,
WITH LOVE

ONCE, THERE WAS A disciple who left home to study with a great teacher. When the student returned, his friends gathered around to ask about the ideas and principles he'd learned. But the disciple replied, "I went to the master to study how he ties his shoes."

That's how I felt about one of my college English professors. He was on the junior faculty, eight years older than I, if that. A tall, bespectacled man with a thatch of sandy hair. I recognized his type from high school, which was still very much part of my undergraduate frame of reference. He would have been one of those shy, awkward, smart boys who were peripheral to the social pecking order but too nice to be considered nerdy.

I took as many classes from him as I could, one per semester. He taught me Dickens, Hawthorne, and how to write so that the thinking showed. Not a flashy take-the-top-of-your-head-off lecturer, he was thorough and thoughtful and well prepared in class. When a student asked a good question, he'd pay serious attention. He engaged. He connected.

I hung around his office whenever I could find an excuse to drop in. I would eavesdrop on his conversations with colleagues, take note of the way he took his coffee, and the tone he used on the phone with his wife. It always felt like a privilege.

I wonder what would happen if I were to show up at his office today, an eager twenty-year-old who does all the reading and wants to talk about ideas over lunch. Would I be welcome to stay? Would I be permitted that easy, leisurely contact with someone who was neither parent nor peer, so I could learn about literature and growing up? I worry that everyone is too wary for that kind of informal intimacy these days. I hope my daughter will find it possible to build on relationships born in the classroom, charged by ideas and the reciprocal pleasure of learning and teaching.

As little children, we love our teachers unabashedly. We bring them presents and cry when it's time to say good-bye in June. Teachers who do not love their students should find other employment.

There are limits, to be sure. There are rules and lines that should never be crossed. Some teachers sexually blackmail their students. Some students seduce their teachers, who should always know better, regardless.

Sexual harassment at the university level is far too common, but it's not the rule. The overwhelming majority of students graduate after twelve, sixteen, or twenty years without a single inappropriate encounter with a teacher. It would be an awful shame if the egregious exceptions were to cost every student—and teacher—something so dear. And while teachers are more cautious than they used to be, my professorial friends assure me that their office doors are still open to the kids who want to hash out ideas or just drink coffee together.

Of course, not all teachers are the mentoring kind, nor do they need to be. The most brilliant lecturer of my college career took no more notice of me than of the flies buzzing in the back of the hall. I didn't care. It was enough that he took the top of my head off.

Besides, I was lucky. I had already found Harry Marten, who taught me about Dickens, and writing, and how to tie my shoes.

DOGS AND KATZ

MY BEAGLE LIVED through fifteen eventful years, accompanying me through college, graduate school, a divorce, remarriage, many jobs, and the indignity of being out-cuted in his own house by a baby.

When Bartholomew died, I lost the guarantee that someone in my house would always be in a good mood. My human family is lovely, but in his absence, I was almost never greeted at the door with a wild outpouring of ardor, gratitude, and unconditional love. Life without him meant that no one was simply dying to lick my toes.

I was dogless, which meant that I went for walks only when the spirit moved me. My check register showed no

entries for the veterinarian. I was free to go away on weekends without worrying about what to do with the pooch.
There was no bowl of water dripping onto the kitchen
floor. My house smelled dogless.

It was too sad.

Canines correct the existential imbalances of human
beings, such as our insatiable need for affection and the constant gratification of our primary sense—which is touch.
Dogs never walk away from petting, patting, scratching, or
stroking. And even when you are momentarily sated, a dog
will put his head in your lap and look up (eyes wet with adoration) for more. No matter how loving your mate, no matter how huggy-kissy your kid, doglessness spells tactile
deprivation.

Dogs are not subtle. They shiver and drool at your touch.
They have no secrets and no false pride as they wait for you
to get down on the floor and play, like a mammal, at last.

After my beloved beagle died, I did experience moments
of guilty relief, especially on frigid mornings and rainy
nights when no one needed walking. But I never once considered parting with his wicker bed or his food and water
bowls. They awaited a successor. I don't like being dogless.
The day I found myself cruising the pet-food aisle at the
supermarket, I knew it was time to fill the bowlegged gap
left by my late hound.

Enter Pom, the poodle.

"A poodle?" they gasped, or sniffed with an air of superior amusement. "You got a *poodle*?"

117

Never mind that he was housebroken within hours, or that his vocabulary is bigger than the average hockey fan's, or that he is as gentle as a lamb. Tell people you've got a poodle, and they tend to react as though you've announced that you breakfast on champagne and bonbons.

Naturally, I get defensive. I rush to explain that ours is a midsize "miniature," not a tiny, yappy "toy," a distinction that is as dishonest as it is disloyal since I have no firsthand experience with high-strung toy poodles. Nor does my quibble convince anyone that I have not somehow sullied my credentials as a regular person.

I can't tell you exactly why I set my heart on a poodle. Poodles (curly-haired, intellectual, leggy) are as different from beagles (flat-coated, stubborn, squat) as canaries and ostriches. Perhaps picking his polar opposite was an unconscious way of paying tribute to the fact that there was no replacement for my First True Dog.

But the whole poodle issue became moot as we all fell in love with Pom. And then I chanced upon a book called *Thurber's Dogs.* Turns out that one of the most curmudgeonly men to inhabit the pages of American literature shared fifteen years of his grumpy life with a purebred poodle named (get this) Christabel. So the next time someone sneers at Pom, I am not going to apologize or temporize. I'm just going to say, "Yeah, we have a poodle, and he's perfectly swell. You wanna make something of it?"

Actually, my passion for poochies has its roots in childhood deprivation. My brother and I begged our parents for a dog. We were given goldfish. We pleaded still harder and got a parakeet. We whined mightily enough to win a pair of short-lived hamsters. But nothing on earth would move my mother to permit a dog. A proud *baleboste*, which is a Yiddish term for "one ferocious homemaker," she viewed dogs and cats with professional horror. From her, I absorbed the idea that Jews don't have pets.

That's nonsense, of course. When my ancestors were shepherds, they depended on dogs to tend their sheep and goats. When my great-great-great-grandparents kept cows and chickens, they relied upon cats to keep the mice in check. And indeed, whenever and wherever Jews have attained a certain level of material comfort—in London or Budapest or Cairo—they kept dachshunds, or Abyssinians, or whatever creature was popular at the time.

The urge to live with animals is a universal human attribute. Where there are people, there are pets, and debates about the relative merits of dogs versus cats. The Talmud (Horayot 13a) asks, "Why does a cat not recognize its master the way a dog does?"

I think that dogs are, constitutionally, Jewish. They whine and they bark. When you leave them alone for long periods of time, they are masters of guilt. They are also, however, very forgiving. And they live to eat.

Dogs are not merely Jewish, they are devout. Every morning, my dog greets me with the fervid happiness of a Hasid. I open my eyes and he responds, "It's you? You're alive! Oh, this is beyond wonderful. I'm alive, too! Seeing

119

you is delightful, thrilling, terrific. I love you!" Dogs
remind us that God considers human beings the crown of
creation.

I am not quite as well versed in the kabala of kitties, but
Judaism contains multitudes of opinions, innumerable
styles, paths, and species. I'm willing to concede that cats
have Jewish lessons to teach. Even though they are, tem-
peramentally, more restrained than most of the human
Jews I've met, cats certainly have as great a claim to piety
as my pooch.

The pleasures provided by cats are intellectual, even
scholarly in the ways they require interpretation. Does
purring imply gratitude? Does a cat purr for the sake of
purring or for the sake of heaven?

Waking up with a feline offers its own profoundly Jewish spiritual lesson. Upon arising, the cat might blink in
your direction to acknowledge your existence. Or not.
Walking into the path of an incoming sunbeam that shows
off her undeniable physical beauty, she tosses her tail as if
to say, "Hey, hotshot, don't kid yourself. The center of the
universe you're not."

TIME ZONES

I HAVE two calendars, one Jewish, one secular, and each has a full complement of holidays and holy days, obligations and celebrations. Living within two time zones can lead to some seriously overbooked weeks, like when Thanksgiving and Hanukkah overlap.

Given the deadlines of magazine writing, I had to get in the mood for any given milestone as much as eight weeks in advance. Writing about Passover in January or Labor Day in July was a little disorienting, but it was also a gift. Preparing for a holiday or a change in the season without having to shop, clean, cook, or travel afforded me a longer view on the start of a new school year or the attainment of a landmark birthday. It was also a solid reminder to pay attention to the tulips or the snow or whatever was happening outside the window at that decidedly fleeting moment.

STRADDLING
THE CALENDAR

EVERY AUTUMN, you can hear the Jews kvetching about the timing of our holidays. Either too early, with Rosh Hashanah, the New Year, hard on the heels of Labor Day. Or too late, so that Yom Kippur—the Day of Atonement, when synagogues are packed to the rafters—coincides with the World Series.

It's not altogether easy living one step outside the Gregorian mainstream. But this is what happens when you live with one foot in the totally predictable solar calendar and the other one planted in the lunar calendar, where no two years are quite the same. To figure out your Thanksgiving travel plans, count four Thursdays and bingo! But to find out when Hanukkah starts, most people need a consultation as well as a date book.

Every year I get at least three phone calls from people asking me when Hanukkah begins. Even though it's marked on most wall calendars, the confusion is understandable because Jewish holidays commence and conclude at sundown, which doesn't quite correlate with the Gregorian system, or the public school system.

Straddling two calendars can lead to occasional muscle strain, but I have to confess that I sort of enjoy the juggling. It makes me stop and remember who I am, where I come from, and how I fit in. One of the main points of all holidays—Simchat Torah, Las Posadas, Diwali, Easter—is to put a stop to time, or at least to the way we take it for granted.

The clock on the wall and the watch on your wrist would have you believe that the hours and years pass by in a constant and undifferentiated stream. We think of time as a force that shapes us but over which we have no control— sort of like gravity. And when we talk about time, it is usually cast as the enemy: the thief that steals youth and vacations in an ever-accelerating getaway car. "Where did the summer go?" we ask. "What happened to November?"

Holidays drop an anchor in time, which, in the words of a dreadful vintage pop tune, "keeps on slippin', slippin', slippin' into the future." Holidays grab time by its invisible hand and invite it to the table, where it seems almost palpable.

Every Christmas is some kind of first. The baby's first taste of cranberry sauce. The first one since the divorce.

Yet on holidays, every first time is also the ultimate experience—the latest in a long line. Holidays open a window on the past, which attends in the shape of memory: Remember the Passover you brought your fiancée home to meet the family? The Easter you forgot to turn on the oven and wound up eating the pies first?

Holidays are not abstract meditations on time, but ritual structures built out of songs, games, family feuds, football, tablecloths, and lots of recipes.

Meals are an integral part of the spell. Great chefs and food writers, even those who are unimpressed with the flavor and texture of turkey, rarely suggest substituting any other main course at Thanksgiving. Repetition makes potent culinary magic, so why mess with it?

Holidays celebrate the repetitive nature of time, its continuities, its cycles. In a nation of immigrants, where change, assimilation, and innovation are cornerstones of the culture, holiday traditions seem especially precious. I have a friend who owns a large collection of Christmas doodads: china Santa figurines, red and green nut cups, candles that are never lighted, centerpieces. She is a little embarrassed to display it all, but her friends ooh and ahh without a trace of irony.

Holidays are respites, giving us the chance to pause and reflect upon all the days we didn't count dear enough. And it's never too early—or late—for that.

ROSH HASHANAH

EVERY YEAR, on the day before Rosh Hashanah, I find myself driving from errand to meeting, trying to remember if I have any honey in the house, if there are apples in the refrigerator, whether I'll find time to bake something for dessert. I get to the bakery on the late side, hoping they'll still have a round challah left for me.

As evening falls, we light the candles and drip honey on the tablecloth. "Happy New Year," I say to Jim. "Shanah tova," I say to Emilia. Kiss, kiss. Eat up. Let's get going so that we can park and get a good seat.

Once we sit down in the sanctuary—and only then—do I begin to get my spiritual house in order. Which is the point of all this hoopla, after all. Days of Awe. Soul search-ing. Like that.

I look around the big room where I got married, where my daughter was named, became bat mitzvah, and gradu-ated from Hebrew high school. I watch and my heart fills, like the room itself.

The sanctuary is never full for this service. Unlike the other High Holidays, a single shift more than accommo-dates the demand. I suppose many people prefer to linger around the table tonight; tomorrow is plenty of time to pray. But I wouldn't miss this one. It's my favorite, and not just because it's the shortest.

For me, the Erev (eve of) Rosh Hashanah service is the most reliable source of religious inspiration of the season. After the vacations and absences of the summer, it's a chance to check out my congregation again. And they look marvelous.

Not only are they dressed up, the positive effects of time spent down on Cape Cod or up in Maine are still in evi-dence. Everyone is smiling. I scan the room and see people who have eaten at my table and people whose names I can never remember, people I see at Torah study on Saturday morning and people I see only at High Holiday services. People who were children last year and who turned into adults over the summer.

The kids knock me out. Not little kids. The evening ser-vice starts at eight-thirty. (As is customary among Reform Jews, you not only eat before services, you have time for a leisurely piece of strudel, too.) So I'm talking about the teenagers.

The change from two-year-old to two-and-a-half may be striking, but it's nowhere near as dramatic as what happens to a twelve-year-old or a fifteen-year-old over the course of a summer. They grow in six-inch spurts. They acquire mustaches. Or they grow breasts. They shake hands like real people. They greet one another like adults, only with much more feeling.

"Jen, you look awesome!"

"Jesse, man, did your parents, like, let you get your ear pierced?"

"Shira! How was camp?"

They sprout wings over the summer. It's clear that they will be leaving us soon.

I not only watch the scene, I make the scene, too. I am kissed and hugged. Someone waves at me from across the room. I catch someone else's eye and we smile at each other. There is a veritable roar of meeting and greeting, of recognition and welcome. Sweeter than honey and apples.

On Erev Rosh Hashanah I remember how good it is to be a part of this congregation, and to be one of this people. I remember how good it is to be alive and how grateful I am to be where I am and nowhere else.

I am smiling. I have tears in my eyes. Now I am ready for the High Holidays, the Days of Awe, the Yamim Noraim.

My rabbi pounds his hand on the podium so hard that

we can hear his ring strike the wood. "Shah!" he roars with a big smile on his face.

It is the birthday of the world every minute. Tonight we come to remember and rejoice. My cantor opens her mouth to sing, and we catch fire.

THE SUKKAH
NEXT DOOR

WHEN I WAS FIRST married, if you had told me there
would ever be a sukkah in my backyard, I would have
scoffed.

Those strange little huts? The ones you see every fall in
synagogue courtyards and outside Orthodox homes? For a
holiday I don't understand and rarely remember? Me? Naah.

But ten years later there it was, sitting on the patio,
already weathered and well used, a masterpiece of lumber-
yard lattice, cinder blocks, and bungee cords. Decorated
with cornstalks and Indian corn, hung with Jewish New
Year cards, it isn't exactly traditional, but it's hard to miss.

Sukkahs are springing up all over the place, aided and abetted by the ever-adaptive American marketplace. Sukkahs have moved so far into the mainstream of the Jewish community that you can purchase the fixings to build your own in hardware stores and Judaica shops all over the country. And don't forget the sukkah websites, which will ship an all-inclusive package (your choice of fiberglass, vinyl, or canvas) anywhere on earth.

Rabbis and Jewish educators have sold the idea of the sukkah to parents of young kids as the great alternative to the Christmas tree. You can string up all the twinkling lights you like inside it, and decorate to your heart's content. And then you can take the sleeping bags out there and spend the night. Grown-ups have taken to the notion of progressive sukkah dinner parties—hors d'oeuvres at the Cohen-Rileys', casseroles at the Millers', and dessert at the Myers'.

Of course, the reality of the sukkah doesn't always live up to the ideal. There have been years when my sukkah sat forlorn in the yard, battered by chilly winds and rains, the greeting cards ruined, the cornstalks rotted. Bundled up in sweaters and gloves, we sometimes managed only one hurried meal within its flimsy walls, feeling foolish and catching cold.

But other years, Indian summer turns our sukkah into an enchanted bower. Late-blooming flowers decorate the table, where breakfast, lunch, and dinner are consumed just a little slower than usual. We bring the oil lamp outside and laughter rises up to the stars that peek through the leaves.

We have some wonderful photographs taken in our sukkah. The table is loaded with a seasonal feast—apple pies, tomatoes in profusion, bottles of wine. Friends crowd together, the kids mugging for the camera. Looking at those pictures, I can almost smell the tang of autumn leaves.

Regardless of the weather, Sukkot is the only harvest celebration that really connects me—an urban Jew for generations—to the rhythms of planting and reaping. By Thanksgiving, it's far too cold to even think of eating outdoors and we're chewing food that was collected weeks ago.

But at Sukkot, I sit in my flimsy booth with a glass of wine, my family and friends, and wonder what I might be doing ten years down the road that seems unthinkable to me today.

ASSIMILATING
THANKSGIVING

THANKSGIVING IS one secular American holiday that Jews have embraced with remarkably little debate or dissent. And why not? There is no Christian rite or ritual associated with it, and gathering the family around the table, giving thanks, and enjoying a huge meal is a patently Jewish activity. Besides, after the autumn avalanche of Jewish holidays, a festive meal without liturgy comes as a relief.

Joan Nathan's book *Jewish Cooking in America* is full of fascinating hints about the Jewish embrace of Thanksgiving. There were Jews who preferred to swallow some American customs whole, as with the Chestnut Stuffing for

Turkey recipe from Mrs. Harriet Meyer, dated 1913. On the other hand, Batsheva Levy Saltzman brought her mother's Moroccan Sukkot pumpkin soup to suburban Boston. A Cuban-Jewish menu from Miami includes not only turkey and cranberry sauce, but plantains, rice, black beans, and stuffed derma.

In my own kitchen, my Armenian-Assyrian-*Mayflower*-Jewish husband takes care of the turkey, using an Italian recipe that calls for a lot of lemon and garlic. This frees me to do one of my favorite things: bake pie.

For most Americans, pie is a standard of ease: things are "nice as pie," or "normal as pie." But as the daughter of immigrants, pie is a pleasure I discovered only in adulthood, making it downright exotic.

My mother, who grew up in Paris, approached American cooking with distrust, if not distaste. Although both my parents were proud citizens of the United States, the food "here" was never up to European standards. There was that terrible salted butter, the disaster of canned vegetables, the hideous cottony stuff passed off as bread. And desserts were almost always way too sweet.

American ingredients and American cooking have improved a lot since I was a child, and even my mother has mellowed in her judgments. To this day, however, she can't abide the taste of cinnamon, which practically constitutes its own food group around Thanksgiving. My liberal use of the quintessentially American spice proves to her that I have become a real, assimilated American.

"Assimilate" has long been a dirty word in the Jewish world. Yet according to my dictionary, it's sweet in the mouth: "to consume and incorporate into the body; to digest. To metabolize constructively. To absorb."

The culinary history of the Jews can be read as a story of triumphant assimilation. The ongoing metabolization of customs, languages, fashions, fruits, nuts, and spices around the world did not give us a single, unified Jewish culture. Instead, it kept us busy creating new recipes and menus for celebrations as old as Passover, as new as the Fourth of July.

On Thanksgiving I assimilate many things my great-grandparents would not understand: grape leaves, turkey stuffed with rice, apple-cranberry pie. I like to think I could win over my ancestors with the aroma and flavors of this truly international, truly American, truly Jewish feast.

At the very least, they would have been reassured by the blessing that accompanies the first glass of wine at our table: *Shehechiyanu*, you have kept us alive; *v'keyamanu*, you have sustained us; *v'higianu lazman hazeh*, you have brought us here. Amen.

CHRISTMAS LESSONS

CHRISTMAS OFFERS American Jews an annual opportunity to grumble, to hide, or to learn from the questions presented us by the biggest national holiday of the year. Exactly how far outside the mainstream am I really? How okay am I with being countercultural? Is it over yet?

Many years ago, I made the joyful discovery that Chinese restaurants are packed on Christmas Eve. Outside, there may be caroling and wassailing and whatever, but inside the Jade Palace (or wherever you go for lo mein and spring rolls), Jewish and Chinese families serenade each other with the happy clatter of domed stainless steel serving dishes.

Another Yule, while walking the dog through a cold

morning, I discovered that Christmas fills the city with the most profound daylight silence of the year. The people are inside, playing with their new stuff, cooking and eating; outdoors, the loudest sound is the rattle of the last, brittle leaves on skeletal trees. It's a deep and peaceful quiet that wraps me in the cocoon of my Jewishness, where I do not feel shut out or angry, but free and light, exempt from the pressure to be merry.

I learned the most about Christmas from my daughter, year after year. When she was three, I noticed how the electric Santa displays in the mall were arrayed at precisely her eye level, and saw how the holiday goodies were clearly targeted to the most vulnerable consumers. When she was four, Emilia announced, "Zack and Christine have Christmas. We have Hanukkah and Shabbat," and I saw how she'd understood that her exclusion from the biggest, snazziest, most kid-seductive event in America was actually part of a reasonable trade-off.

But when Emilia was six, she stamped her foot and said, "I hate Christmas lights." They reminded her that she was an outsider, which doesn't feel good in kindergarten. No amount of arguing could convince her of the obvious beauty of the colorful, twinkling, flickering little bulbs, so I learned to shut up and let her be angry.

A few years later while we were shopping at the mall, a gray-haired woman behind the pharmacy counter beamed at my daughter and asked, "Do you know what Santa is going to bring you?"

Emilia blinked her blue eyes at the nice lady and politely explained, "We don't celebrate Christmas. We're Jewish."

I held my breath. Would the woman be offended? Would sword-bearing Cossacks swoop down from between the tinseled forests of Aisle 3: "Seasonal"?

"Well!" said the woman, surprised but smiling. "You have a happy holiday."

"Happy holiday," said Emilia, perfectly oblivious to the freighted past I schlepped with me. She smiled and accepted her change, just a Jewish-American kid doing business at Christmastime. No biggie.

HA-HA-HANUKKAH

WEEKS BEFORE Thanksgiving, my neighborhood stationery store put up a display of Hanukkah cups and paper plates, Hanukkah banners and streamers, Hanukkah stained-glass-window kits and sand-art kits, Hanukkah pencils, erasers, pads of paper, stickers for the window, coloring books and color-in posters. This is not a Judaica shop by any means, but in my one-third-Jewish neighborhood, the place was stocked with dreidels that whistle, dreidels that walk, dreidels made of wood, glass, brass, and plastic. The big hollow plastic dreidels are for filling with gold-paper-covered chocolate gelt (money) in a choice of dark, milk, low-fat, or white.

The store owner was actually apologetic about the amount of space he'd allotted for Hanukkah cards; the Christmas stuff would dwarf it all, he said. But I was overwhelmed by the selection. I counted more than fifty different cards, including racy ones ("Rabbi Claustein, is it kosher to have sex on Hanukkah?"), cutesy-pie ones (giddy mice prancing around menorahs), and punny ones ("Wishing you the 'oys' of the season").

A mile away, the big-box home goods store had even more stuff. The shelves groaned with blue and white linen tablecloths and matching napkins; pot holders and dish towels with a menorah motif; coffee mugs and serving platters hand-painted with six-pointed stars. I counted three different kinds of imported, long-burning Hanukkah candles, electric menorahs (with three-tone bulbs, sold separately), and marzipan candies made in the shapes of teeny challahs and menorahs.

"America *ganef*," my grandmother would have said, with a snort and a shake of her head. Ganef means "thief," but in this context it's a half-grudging compliment to American entrepreneurship: you can make money off anything in this country. Hey, if Halloween can become a multimillion-dollar seasonal industry, why not Hanukkah?

Jewish purists object to the marketing of what they insist upon calling "a minor holiday." Compared with Passover or even Sukkot, Hanukkah is small potatoes. To those who bemoan the Yule-ification of our modest, happy festival of lights, I say, "Relax." Why not dress up the house with things that twinkle and shine? When you live in latitudes where the sun sets at 4 P.M., where the nights are bitter as well as long, a little tinsel goes a long way.

This is not about competing with Christmas; we'll never match the sheer wattage, nor is that the point. The point is an entirely Jewish one called *hiddur mitzvah*—the rabbinic admonition that we make our Jewish lives beautiful.

So while I'm kind of grossed out by the Mickey Mouse menorahs, I am still frustrated in my search for a string of graceful, well-designed Hanukkah lights. America *ganef*, get on the stick! After all, you sold me on the electric menorah.

I used to scoff at them. I thought they were tacky, or for people too fastidious or neurotic or lazy to enjoy the real thing—hot and dripping and a little dangerous. It was the danger that finally got me to reconsider my opposition to plugging in, and I've become a fan of the all-night light.

I used to put wax candles in the window, where they could be seen, albeit briefly, from outside the house. Placing the Hanukkah menorah where it can cast its light into the darkness is one of the most important mitzvot (sacred obligations) of the holiday. We're supposed to "proclaim the miracle" of Hanukkah to the world.

I've never been impressed by or convinced of the holiday's official story, about a small quantity of oil—only enough for a single day—that burned for eight when the Temple in Jerusalem was restored by the Maccabees after its desecration by Syrian-Greek occupiers. I commemorate another miracle when I set the candles in the window. After all, in a single generation, the Jews of my family have gone from hunted and hiding in Europe to public and proud in America.

But even in America, putting Jewish lights in plain sight requires taking a deep breath. In 1993, rocks shattered a child's menorah-bedecked bedroom window in Billings, Montana; the resurgence of international anti-Semitism, post–September 11, looms in the background. That said, the ongoing marvel of Jewish survival still merits my modest acclaim.

It helps having company in making this little leap of faith. Every year, there are more houses with electric menorahs in the window. I look for them as I drive on side streets and busy thoroughfares, reassured and cheered to see them burning, proclaiming, celebrating.

Still and all, we don't sing the blessings and songs when we screw in the pointy little bulbs of the electric menorah. Those we save for the "real" one—warm and brief. With wax and flame, we create a kind of hearth, small but bright enough to banish the gloom. Miraculous.

PURIM ROCKS

PURIM IS THE PREMIERE pediatric Jewish observance in America, which is too bad. The tots are adorable, dressed up as Esther and the King, lining up for the ring toss and trinkets at the synagogue Purim carnival. But the truth is, Purim is wasted on the young.

It sure didn't start out as a kiddie event. The Jewish version of Mardi Gras—complete with foolishness, license, and excess—it is based upon the Book of Esther, an R-rated burlesque full of drunkenness, harem sexuality, and violence. And then there's the fact that we're supposed to get falling-down, drooling, stupid drunk on Purim. Too drunk to tell the difference between Mahatma Gandhi and Osama bin Laden. That drunk. Purim gives permission for cross-dressing and gambling, too. Purim means "lots," as in "Bet the whole lot on red."

Purim can certainly accommodate cute kids, but it requires grown-ups to cavort and giggle, to sing the hymn "Adon Olam" to the tune of "I've Been Working on the Railroad." To read *Mad Magazine* in the sanctuary and look up the jokes in the Talmud. Bava Batra 23b and Berachot 8b. I kid you not.

Best of all, this foolishness is the stuff of religious devotion. Once a year, Purim comes along to tell Jews to stop posing as a nation of priests, to wipe the smirk off our collective faces, replace it with an idiotic grin and get down and boogie with You-Know-Who, Who certainly digs Purim. How else do you explain the traditional belief that Purim—not Yom Kippur, not even Passover—will be the only holiday celebrated *after* the messiah arrives?

This is very good news. I've often wondered if paradise might not be, well, boring. God must know how badly we need to laugh at ourselves. And if Purim is a keeper even in a fully redeemed, peaceful, just world, maybe the world to come will turn out to be a friendly asylum staffed by the Marx Brothers, Molly Picon, Henny Youngman, and Lenny Bruce—whose collective memory is a riot.

This is serious nonsense! If your rabbi doesn't deliver a creditable sermon on Yom Kippur, your rabbi will probably get the boot. Likewise, if your rabbi doesn't do a disreputable funky chicken on Purim, your rabbi ought to get the hook.

So slip that seltzer bottle up your sleeve. Put on your high-heeled sneakers. Take my tsuris, please.

THE ORANGE ON THE
SEDER PLATE

EVERY JEWISH FAMILY produces a unique version of the Passover seder—the big ritual meal of traditional foods, served after and amid liturgy, storytelling, and song. We're all surprised at each other's customs: You eat lamb? You don't sing "Chad Gad Ya"?

And yet, virtually every seder does share a few common elements. Matzoh crumbs all over the floor. Wine stains on the tablecloth. A seder plate containing the traditional symbols of the holiday: a roasted shank bone and hard-boiled egg, recalling the days of the Temple sacrifices; horseradish and salt water for the bitterness of oppression;

parsley for spring; *haroset,* a mixture of wine, nuts, and fruit symbolizing mortar and the heavy labor performed by the Israelite slaves.

And for lots of us, an orange.

The ancient Hebrews who fled into the wilderness didn't know from citrus fruit, and there certainly weren't any Valencias on Grandma's seder plate. Starting in the 1980s, the new holiday symbol has been showing up on an ever-increasing number of Passover tables.

The custom originated with the teacher and writer Susannah Heschel, who first set it out as a symbol of inclusion for lesbian and gay Jews, and in following years for all those who have been marginalized in the Jewish community. Thanks largely to the Internet, Jewish women adopted the fruit as symbol of their inclusion, and now there are oranges on seder plates all over the world, as well as alternative stories about how they got there in the first place.

Regardless of its genesis, that orange now makes several subtle spiritual and political statements. For one thing, it represents the creative piety of liberal Jews, who honor tradition by adding new elements to the old. The orange also announces that those on the margins have fully arrived as coauthors of Jewish history, as does the presence of another new ritual item, the Miriam's Cup, which acknowledges the role of Moses' sister, the singer-songwriter-prophet, in the story.

The orange is a living part of the ancient pedagogic

strategy of Passover. We are commanded to teach our children about the Exodus from Egypt in a manner so vivid that everyone at the table—but especially the kids—remembers (not merely imagines but actually remembers) what it feels like to be a hungry, hunted slave. The seder makes memory manifest, tangible, and solid as Grandpa's kiddush cup.

Just like the shank bone, the orange is there so that someone under the age of thirteen will ask, "What's that thing doing on the seder plate?"

The orange is there so that Mom or Dad can say, "I'm so glad you asked that question. The orange is a symbol of the struggle by Jews who used to be ignored by our tradition—like gays and lesbians, and women, and Jews by choice—to become full partners in religious and community life. The orange is a sign of change, too, because now all kinds of Jews are rabbis and cantors and teachers and leaders. And the orange is a mark of our confidence in the Jewish future, which means that someday maybe you too will bring something new to the seder plate."

The orange on the seder plate is both a playful and a reverent symbol of Judaism's ability to adapt and thrive. It also celebrates the abundant diversity of creation. After all, God, who made the heavens and the earth, and dinosaurs and lemurs and human beings, is clearly a lover of variety and change—not to mention oranges.

YOM HASHOAH

EVERY YEAR, I think about going to the service for Yom HaShoah, Holocaust Remembrance Day. After all, I am the daughter of survivors. This is about my family. This is for me. And I usually go, but not always.

The service tends to be brief. Six yahrzeit (annual memorial) candles flicker on the *bimah*. The *Amidah*, the standing personal prayer, is replaced by six minutes of silence. The mourner's Kaddish prayer is interspersed with the names of concentration camps.

In keeping with the custom of not singing or playing music at Jewish funerals, there was some discussion at my temple about whether it was appropriate for the choral group to participate. Ultimately, a few brief songs were permitted, and the minor-key music does not seem out of place. But the Yom HaShoah service does feel like a funeral. It is, in a way, the funeral my uncle, murdered in Auschwitz, never got. My uncle times six million.

I met a man once who put together a book containing six million sixes. Page after page, filled with nothing but the number six. It was a peculiar volume, enormous, mute, and terrible.

I should go to Yom HaShoah services. Maybe the reason I don't always attend has something to do with God. I do not believe in a personal deity of the sort who rewards and punishes, who watches the sparrow and took a nap on the seventh day. This does not stop me from using the language of the prayer book during the rest of the year. I know what to do with metaphors and I value the restorative power of shared meditation and song.

But by the light of six yahrzeit candles, the words stop me the way they stopped my father. "You redeem us from the hand of oppressors, save us from the grasp of tyrants"— my father used to shake his head. My mother still mutters, "Huh."

Maybe it's better to think of Yom HaShoah services simply as an affirmation of our promise never to forget. It is unimaginable to me that Jews would ever forget this agony of loss, documented in such vivid, visual detail. The memory of that horror seems so much with us, transformed into searing new stories, movies, poems, paintings, music. More every year.

I'm grateful for this artistic grappling because liturgy cannot contain the howl of the Holocaust. At least, not yet.

I wonder what Yom HaShoah will look like in a hundred generations. Will it look like Passover? The crown of all our holidays—joyful, thoughtful, and a culinary delight—is grounded in the ancient horror of four hundred years in slavery. We make a celebration out of our freedom by reminding ourselves, "We were slaves in Egypt."

Or will it look like Tishah b'Av, a day of mourning for the destruction of the Temple in the year 70, a holy day that goes ignored by the vast majority of American Jews? There is no debate about the historical reality of the razing of the Jerusalem Temple, which was the center of the Jewish universe. Judaism was utterly transformed by that cataclysm: no more priests, no more sacrifices, no more central address or holy sites. Just the memories and a book.

The formal commemoration of Yom HaShoah is like a recent widow, wailing in the darkness. For now, six burning candles and six silent minutes are the best we can muster to remind us that everyone is a survivor and that memory is a sacred trust.

YAHRZEIT

YAHRZEIT MEANS "year's time," and it refers to the anniversary of a loved one's death. For me, all of August is my father's yahrzeit, the month in which he not only died, but was born, too.

It was August the year the U.S. team won the women's World Cup in soccer, and every time I saw a headline about the games or watched some of the action on TV, my dad was with me. He would have gotten such a charge out of it. Although he was hardly a sports fan, he'd played soccer as a boy in Germany and Italy. So on the rare occasions that the networks deigned to show a game from abroad, he would be glued to the set, chortling over the athletic prowess of the wiry, long-winded runners who were, in his opinion, so clearly superior to America's muscle-bound football stars.

I remember him watching one such match with his brothers, glasses of red wine in hand, shouting in Italian over the blandishments of the announcer.

My father loved the Italian language more than he loved soccer. His delight in the meaning and texture of words—in any of the four tongues he spoke—was a big part of my childhood. He would pick up a random English word like a geologist who just happened across a perfect quartz and hold it up for me to admire. "Unctuousness." "Femur." "Snoot." He thought "snoot" was a riot.

Even in death, my father continued to be my teacher. Grief is an inescapable human experience. If we live long enough, there isn't any choice in the matter; we are bound to lose people we love. However, we do have a choice in how we grieve, and after my father died, I learned how Jews make those choices. The structure of mourning provided me a path through dark days, from the first week at home to the first month apart to a year of reciting Kaddish—the memorial prayer. It's a path worn smooth by centuries of mourners who walked it before me.

On the anniversary of his death, I light a memorial candle, and Emilia, Jim, and I stop to look at the light and share memories of him. We go to the synagogue and I call out his name and recite Kaddish for him with my congregation. I renew his/our membership in Amnesty International.

My father would have been pleased by these memorials. And he would have gotten a kick out of the way that he continued to expand my vocabulary even after he died: *shloshim,* "the first month"; *kevod ha-met,* "honoring the dead"; *nichum avelim,* "comforting the mourner."

But the word I now understand more deeply every August is the English "blessing." My father's memory is a palpable blessing in my life. It surfaces now and then, an unbidden gift, like a fish leaping up out of a placid lake. So it happens that when I marvel at the ability of the human body to run for ninety minutes without apparent distress, or listen to a Beethoven symphony, or laugh at a shaggy-dog story, my father's face appears in my mind's eye and I am blessed.

IN THE MIDDLE

I T'S HARD to accept that you are, once and for all, a grown-up. Every now and then, I'm still amazed that they let me drive in rush hour.

But the fact is, there is no "they" anymore. I am the "they" that's in charge. I'm in the middle of my life and there is no more waiting for things to begin.

There isn't a whole lot of attention paid to life in the middle, even though the middle is such a long swath of life. It's both the time to remember and the time to plan. The time to grieve and the time to savor. The time to reap and the time to grow.

MIDLIFE,
THE BEGINNING

MUCH ABOUT MIDLIFE is predictable. I'm not surprised by how busy it is, what with mortgages, car pools,
and gum surgery. There's not enough time to exercise or
read.

But I think I expected to find a certain amount of calm
in this stretch of road. Aren't the years between the forties
and sixties supposed to be a period of consolidation, of digging in, of sailing before the wind? But among the midlife
people I know—and the others about whom we gossip—
nearly every man and woman is either dreaming about a
life change or making one happen.

I'm not talking about the mythical "midlife crisis," which the psychologists have pretty much debunked. The folks of whom I speak aren't (for the most part) melting down their marriages, buying bank-busting sports cars, and/or running off to start a new life in an adobe out West.

The changes I've encountered are far less photogenic and not quite so dramatic, but they are substantial and, in their own ways, exciting. M. sold his interest in a business he'd started in order to run a religious school. J. is taking watercolor classes and painting every weekend. R., a sociology professor, is writing mysteries.

Dr. P. is learning to play the flute. L. pruned back a thriving therapy practice to get a night-school graduate degree that will allow her to teach high school history.

These are not people with too much time on their hands or deep pockets. Middle-class folks with a relatively high degree of mastery over their lives, they are simply in search of a good kick in the pants. To a person, they report feeling better than they have in years.

The prelude to these changes isn't always pretty. Midlife review can feel like existential indigestion. "Is this it?" you ask yourself. "I hate my job," you say, but quietly so no one will fire you. The prechange mode may even seem like adolescence revisited, except now you have a couple of people depending on you for groceries.

The need for a midlife jump-start may be part of the human condition. At least that's what developmental psychologist Erik Erikson theorized. According to Erikson, adults face a fundamental choice between "generativity" and "stagnation." Either you start playing the piano, tutor a child in math, or learn a new vocabulary (city planning, perennials, French), or you risk feeling trapped, squashed, finished.

It's hard to imagine what Erikson's theory would have meant to people in 1900, when the average life expectancy was forty-seven years. In 1932—after the introduction of penicillin, improved sanitation, and other mundane miracles—sixty-seven was considered a ripe old age and the number-one nonfiction bestseller was Walter B. Pitkin's chirpy *Life Begins at Forty*.

With life expectancies currently in the eighties (for white women, at least), the John D. and Catherine T. MacArthur Foundation is financing the Research Network on Successful Midlife Development, an international project that seeks to discover nothing less than the foundation of adult satisfaction—or, in foundationese, "the biomedical, psychological, and social factors that permit some people to achieve . . . happiness."

The fact that this project coincides precisely with the graying of the baby boom generation is no coincidence. The most entitled, self-conscious, and best-educated cohort in the history of the world can reasonably expect to be the longest-lived, too. With thirty to forty more years facing many of the middle-aged, it's no wonder there's a rush on second careers, avocations, quests for meaning.

At forty, I took up yoga and writing fiction. Next on my agenda: voice lessons, tap dancing (or maybe flamenco), and building a new kind of mikveh—the Jewish ritual bath. Not necessarily in that order.

FIRST FLAME

THE BABY MEMORY book records the date of my daughter's first step, first word, first encounter with a dog, first trip on an airplane. But once she reached the ripeness of four, we pretty much stopped making entries in the book.

It's not that the firsts stopped. They came at a dizzying pace: our daughter's first attempt at joke telling, first Barbie doll, first trip to the emergency room, first four-letter word, first boyfriend, first heartbreak, first flat tire.

Adulthood has plenty of firsts, too. The big ones are called milestones and they get memorialized at city hall and in the family photo album. First marriage. Firstborn. First home.

For the most part, though, grown-up firsts are modest events that pass uncelebrated, unrecorded, unconsciously, even; the first time you eat quail, or attend an opening-night performance, or buy yourself liniment. But every now and then there's a first like the ones that opened your eyes wide in childhood—like that trip to the Grand Canyon, or Grandma's funeral. Like the time I witnessed my first fire.

It was not a giant conflagration, even though fire trucks from three neighboring cities and one hundred firefighters were on the scene. It didn't make the television news and rated only a few paragraphs of newsprint because there were, thank God, no fatalities.

It may have been the end of the world for the thirty people left homeless in the dead of winter, but in the grand scheme of things, a four-alarm fire in a four-story apartment building would not have caught my attention had I not been riding past just as the third, fourth, and fifth fire trucks pulled in. Or had it been raining. Or had the friend who was driving not pulled the car over, so we could get out for a better look at the biggest flames either of us had ever seen.

Not that anyone alive today is totally unscorched. After the Holocaust, the Blitz, the Bomb, September 11, we all know what hell smells like and how near it lurks. But it is something else again to have your whole face baked, to have your field of vision filled with roaring orange flames, to watch sparks spin like sunlight on water, like fireworks, like hallucinations, and then to startle at the danger of cinders as big as a cat, blowing right at you. It was like watching a storm over the ocean, the power inconceivable yet palpable, deafening, acrid, bright, hot, big, intoxicating, and wickedly awesome.

I caught sight of my first "sparks" in the crowd, too—guys who listen to their citizens band radios and follow the pyrotechnics. But most of the people behind the barricade came from the immediate neighborhood. A small woman kept asking a tall, thin man holding a baby, "Is that our apartment? Is that our apartment?" The firefighters moved quickly, unperturbed by the growing audience whose collective face was turned upward, its conversations respectfully muted.

Everyone murmured admiration for the men climbing through the smoke in their slickers and hats. Dozens of fingers pointed at the man shooting water down through the roof while being drenched by the torrents aimed upward. Two firefighters were taken to the hospital, but both were eventually released and slept in their own beds that night.

The day after the blaze, falling snow hushed the street as drivers slowed to look at the wreckage. The street was littered with glass and sawdust. The windows were already boarded up.

There is no mention of fire in the story of the Garden of Eden. Those two had no need to cook, or to stave off a chill, or to forge a lock for the front door. Fire became necessary only after they took the bait.

We domesticated it in hearths and internal-combustion machines. Children are not permitted to play with it, and we take precautions against its true nature, which is not hostile, simply heartless.

In the week after my first fire, I checked all the smoke alarms in the house, and got some new ones. And we had our first fire drill.

VIGIL

I'M SITTING AT my desk. The computer is humming. My coffee is still hot. The phone rings. It's God.

"Excuse me," says God, "I know you are busy with your life, your work, your child. I know your schedule is tight. But I want you to drop everything, get into an airplane, and spend a week in a windowless room with a bunch of strangers. There, in semidarkness, you will sit and wonder whether your father is going to live or die."

Inside the intensive-care waiting room, you sit with empty hands. You never fully catch your breath. You go to the cafeteria sometimes because you have to, but mostly your mouth is busy chewing over bits of information (the blood gasses look okay, his temperature hasn't gone up). It is something to talk about, but there is as little nourishment or relief in those morsels as there is air in the waiting room.

There are pillows in the waiting room, but there is no rest. There are magazines on the tables, but there is no reading. Your mind jumps from hope to despair, from planning a home-care strategy for when he gets better to anticipating the memorial service. You remember the sweetest things.

I must have been seven or eight years old when he read novels to me and my brother at bedtime, a chapter a night. The books were often way over our heads. I'm pretty sure that once he read us *The Sea-Wolf* by Jack London. Every night, we learned new words.

I remember one night when he tucked me in, he said something about the fact that someday he wouldn't be around anymore. A few moments later I was in his arms, sobbing. He smiled at me and said, "I knew the minute I said that, I shouldn't have." He reassured me that he was going to be around for a long, long time and not to worry.

In the waiting room I wonder if he recalls that story. He is always so surprised by what I dredge up from my childhood. "The things you remember!" he exclaims.

Now that I'm a parent, I know how little I remember of the care, pride, and worry that he and my mother lavished on me and my brother. My daughter will likewise remember little from her earliest years, which were so vivid for me. I will tell her about her first jokes, her first friends, but I won't be able to describe the texture of these days, too lovely for words.

Words fail so many strong feelings, which is why, I suppose, no one ever tried to tell me what it's like to see your daddy draped with plastic tubing, fighting for breath, his hands searching for a nonexistent pocket in his sleep, nearly naked under the hospital sheet.

Guarding the electric doors to the ICU are dragons wearing pink smocks. They are white-haired ladies, most of them, volunteers who smile a lot. We who sit in the waiting room hate them. We call them names behind their back and shoot poison darts at them with our eyes, even when we ask for favors.

One of those pink dragons told me she didn't know how we could stand it in the waiting room, with so many people around all the time.

Actually, it helps. You cannot sit, endlessly remembering, worrying, fighting fear of the worst with hope for the best. Adult tears are so debilitating. Who knows how long you're going to be waiting? You have to marshal your strength. So other people provide distraction as well as a tacit fellowship. Sometimes you trade information: How old is he? What did the doctor say?

Mostly, though, you just watch them cope. Poor Mrs. P., whose father seemed never to improve; when her husband finally showed up, he was falling-down drunk and we all averted our eyes. When Mr. C. was transferred to a medical floor, there was a great stir as members of his big family collected their papers and bags. We all watched their relief, envious.

There was a death, too: a twenty-year-old kid was shot in the chest in the middle of the night. His relatives did not come into the waiting room but went directly into the Awful Room, a small antechamber across the hall. We heard them keening.

Nothing is quite the same after this. Not even if there is a recovery and a discharge home. There is no hope of ever again knowing that sense of complete safety you felt as a child, when you slept knowing that Daddy and Mommy were watching out. Before that phone call, there was a whole generation between you and death. Now, there is no one to protect you against the night.

TIME-OUT

"IS THERE SOMETHING you aren't telling me?" asked a
friend when I told her I had spent a weekend at a retreat
center.

No, I assured her. I had no religious conversion to
report. It was just a two-day holiday in the country, an
escape from the telephone and the kitchen. A place to get
a massage, take some yoga classes, and work out the kinks
that come from too much typing.

But as much as I made it sound like no big deal, it
wasn't simply a vacation. It was my first retreat.

"Retreat" is one of those wonderful words that refract
meaning, the way a crystal parses light. Verb and noun,

retreat is as practical as a wily chess move, as spiritual as a monastery full of silent penitents. In a full-steam-ahead culture, retreat tends to be equated too much with defeat and too little with second winds and second chances.

Even so, the notion of withdrawing from the world is pretty foreign to me. It runs counter to my personality, politics, and ethnicity. The way I was raised, the path to God, love, peace, and redemption is other people. As many as possible.

But something in me needed a retreat. Even the most relaxing vacation—say, two weeks reading novels on a quiet beach—involves an expectation of fun. I didn't need fun. I needed to get empty, to squeeze the residue of everyday life out of the saturated sponge of my gray matter. And so, it seemed, did three hundred other people who were lodged with me in the Jesuit-seminary-turned-yoga-center in the Berkshires.

What attracted me to that particular weekend package rather than a couple of nights in a charming country inn was the chance to practice yoga, which I'd just begun to study.

Yoga appeals on many levels. Just the names of the poses suggest a surpassing, inanimate calm: Mountain, Reed, Tree, even Corpse. Of course, there are other postures, such as Warrior and Child, which require an effort of the spirit as well as the hamstrings. The Warrior is strategic and purposeful as a general's battlefield retreat. To the military mind, falling back doesn't necessarily signify loss; it's a technique that permits regrouping and resupply so you can rejoin the fray and prevail.

In the Child pose, you kneel and fold yourself over into the smallest possible space. It is dark inside this posture and safe enough for tears, helpless giggling, naps, and longing to be held until you're all better.

My fellow retreatants included nurses and ministers, waiters and teachers, all come to stretch, bend, and let go a little of the too-muchness. In the busy-quiet hallways and gardens, there was a sense of purpose, not work. Of motion, not rush. Of relief.

The weekend passed through me and over me, too quickly, but completely. I slept enough. I thought only a little. I quieted a lot. I'll go back.

Just before getting into the car to head home, I paused on the terrace to memorize the gorgeous green bowl of the valley below, when the sound of a woman sobbing poured out from a window. The uncensored crying of an adult is an unsettling, almost dangerous sound. Like an approaching avalanche, with a painful, dredged-up weight to every breath. But it also resembles uncontrollable laughter. It reminded me of the cries in labor and delivery.

In another place, that woman's sobs would have seemed terrible and troubling, a call for help. But there, in retreat, they seemed like part of the business at hand. I knew she would feel better afterward. It had been a long time since I had cried, too.

GOOD-BYE

THE CEREMONY AT graveside lasted no more than a few minutes. The drive to the cemetery had been much longer. After we gathered around the coffin, the minister said a few words and poured ashes in the shape of a cross on top of the casket. The funeral director said we could take a flower in remembrance. Then we left.

The coffin stood aboveground, almost floating in the freezing morning. As we drove away, it followed me in the rearview mirror, a burnished-metal memory.

It was bitter cold out there—no trees to break the wind. Even so, I wish I had stayed to see the workmen come with their truckload of soil that would tuck him into the earth.

I would have added my flower to that blanket, burying him just a little.

But that was not the custom of my friend's people, for whom the grave is not seen as final. The spiritual farewell had been taken in the church. There was no point, from their perspective, in dwelling on the physical. Besides, the family seemed comforted, and that's what mattered most.

Years ago, the priest at my Catholic aunt's funeral had gently invited us to leave after the graveside service was concluded. Most people had started moving away, but my aunt's mother—over eighty and mourning her only child—refused to go. Someone moved the Astroturf carpet off the pile of earth near the coffin, and my aunt's mother, wailing, filled her hands with red Georgia clay and emptied it into her daughter's grave.

Death is always a strange country. In Borneo, the climax of the ceremony for the dead involves the singing of special songs to direct the departed spirit on the right path. For the Nyakyusa people of Tanzania, dancing and flirting are part of the ritual. It is only in America that embalming is so widely practiced, and in this country, we need books to teach us how to mourn and grieve.

I was reading about funeral customs at the library. Lifting my eyes from my stack of books, I noticed the gravestones in the cemetery next door. Neatly clipped bushes flanked many of the granite headstones, like evergreen sentinels. It was too cold for flowers. I realized I would probably never return to the cemetery where I'd left my friend. It's a two-hour drive from my home, so it's unlikely that I will ever see the headstone. I won't leave a pebble on it as a token of remembrance. I will always remember him, but I won't visit.

I go to other cemeteries where I don't know a soul. The flowering trees in the Mount Auburn Cemetery draw thousands of us every spring. We walk the hills, and, even though we're not supposed to, bring lunch and picnic on the grass. Couples hold hands. When I was pregnant, I searched the tombstones for interesting names. A year later, my friend and I brought our babies for a stroll. It did not feel disrespectful to be so alive among those long-buried dead.

I remember putting the yellow chrysanthemum from my friend's funeral on the kitchen table, where it held its petals for a week. Every now and then it struck me as odd: a flower from a mortuary arrangement in the room where I eat my cornflakes, answer the phone, read the mail, bake the chicken, wash the dishes.

But more often it just reminded me to think about David's life: his devotion to his friends, the way he learned to love garlic after a heart attack put an end to his relationship with salt, the many times we'd gone to see animated movies together.

When the flower finally lost its last petal, I put a fresh one in the vase.

Heaven on Earth

THERE ARE RASPBERRIES in heaven. In fact, up i
heaven, raspberries are so plentiful and cheap that God an
the angels take them for granted. After dinner the hea
enly hosts say things like "Raspberries and cream f
dessert?"

"No, thanks," reply the cherubs. "We've been snacki
on them all afternoon."

Nutritionally, there may be a more perfect food, bu
every other regard, nothing else comes close. I am spe
ing of red raspberries, of course, furry rubies, cavia
fruits. In the supermarket, they are packaged in puny, l
pint containers that can cost as much as a deli sandwicl

179

the chill of the produce section, where the plastic wrap obscures their velvet and aroma, I can walk past them without turning a hair. But at the farmers' market, where they are heaped in warm, open pints, I am undone and there is no price I won't pay.

Tiny beaded lanterns, the color of a heart newly fallen in love—the architecture of the raspberry is precise and geometric, yet tender. There is even a specific, funny name for its succulent subdivisions: drupelets. A raspberry is a crust of drupelets clustered around an empty cup. The celestial harvest hangs on bushes called brambles, in honor of their defensive thorns.

There must have been raspberries in the Garden of Eden, which convinces me that Adam and Eve were, developmentally at least, nothing but babies. Because given the choice between an apple and an unlimited supply of raspberries, only a small child would go for the Red Delicious.

I know this for a fact because I once accompanied a class of three-year-olds to a pick-your-own farm where there were berries on the brambles and apples on the boughs. The children did not have any patience for the thimble-size berries, which, after an eternal minute's worth of picking, did not even cover the bottom of their paper boxes. The children much preferred the apples, fat prizes hung low enough to accommodate their modest reach. And they went absolutely nuts in the field of pumpkins, where they romped like a bunch of pixies in a Kodak commercial. Meanwhile, I munched happily on their forgotten raspberries.

Berries, the whole lot of them, are exemplary things: concentrated pleasure, complete and cute. As with grapes, which are equally cunning but jollier in the way they explode between your teeth, the extreme edibility of berries—outside and in—invites you to make a direct line between hand and mouth.

So the idea of cooking raspberries seems almost criminal—although they are very fashionable swimming in sauces with game birds, or in puddles around chocolate cake. There are sound arguments to be made for raspberry jam, which has undeniably restorative powers on cold mornings when the memory of "pick your own" days can make you weep.

But the words "raw raspberries" back-to-back demonstrate how absurd it is to apply heat to something so eager to be eaten as is. Raspberries are the most fragile of foods. Even a thoughtless word can bruise them. Once ripe, they are in a rush to be consumed—but not too cold. Never, never right out of the refrigerator.

I once stood in the walk-in cooler of a restaurant when a local grower showed up with boxes of just-picked raspberries for that evening's dessert. The man was not a farmer, it turned out, just a retired gentleman with a big old raspberry patch. I stared at the fellow with the amazing surfeit; more than enough to eat, more than enough to jelly—enough to sell the leftovers for cash.

It seemed like such fantastic wealth, such extravagant luxury. And, even though the darned things grow wild on nearly every continent, it has always seemed so. In the presidential campaign of 1840, Martin Van Buren was viciously attacked for wallowing lasciviously in raspberries. What a delicious image.

What would it be like if we could all roll around in tubs of raspberries? What if those ruby velvet cuplets were as common on earth as they are in heaven—as ordinary as apples, and just as cheap? Would we chop them up thoughtlessly, mere filler for the fruit salad? Would September's summer days seem as wistful?

Despite their ephemerality and downy sensuality, however, I have never heard raspberries called an aphrodisiac. They do not make you want to do anything but eat more raspberries. Which makes them truly paradisiacal.

Raspberries remind you, without any recourse to reason, that paradise is visible, touchable, and tasteable. Paradise is present, provided that you don't just toss a handful into your mouth and gobble it down without feeling its almost imperceptible crush, without savoring the fragrance as the rosy juice dribbles sweetly by and by.

THE COMMUNAL ROUTE

IT'S NOT SO BAD being part of an elephant inside a python. That's the poetic description—shamelessly lifted from Antoine de Saint-Exupéry's *The Little Prince*—applied to the demographic bulge known as the baby boom, of which I am a card-carrying member. By virtue of being born between 1946 and 1964, 78 million of us are a gigantic market if not a movement. Whatever we do or don't do matters now and for decades to come.

In most ways, I look forward to inching my way through the innards of the python warmed by the mass of my peers, forty-something giving way to fifty-, sixty-, and seventy-something. Menopause is big business. Yoga is booming.

I'm anticipating a bunch of unfortunate new buzz-words: "IRAnians" (people living off individual retire-ment accounts), "matriarchies" (look at the actuarial tables), "marijuana-Nana" (glaucoma and nostalgia will create a juggernaut for legalization).

And I'm going to live in a commune. No, not a retire-ment community, but a white-haired version of the way we were in the 1970s, when many of us shared kitchens, bathrooms, and television sets with unrelated roommates. Sometimes it was a royal pain in the neck, as in Who Ate the Oreos? But it was also good knowing that tea would be brewing when you got to a home you could actually afford.

My friends and I have begun to discuss the rules for our geezer collective: no rocking chairs, no conversation about bodily functions at the dinner table, no hair nets, no cigars. "Discussed" isn't really the right way to describe these con-versations: we've laughed ourselves silly. Which is really the long-term goal.

Early plans call for about a half-dozen people (couples and/or an inevitable collection of widows) to pool resources from sales of our various residences. With that money, we'll retrofit a big house with plenty of bathrooms and a chair-lift at the stairs. We'll chip in for housecleaning and snow shoveling, wrangle group rates for first-run plays and a weekly masseuse, on-site. We'll take turns cooking, driving to the health club, planning trips and outings, and chairing house meetings.

The benefits of such an arrangement are obvious. Not

only will we raise our material standard of living (maybe we'll buy a winter retreat in Greece), we'll be protecting ourselves against the great threats of old age: loneliness, isolation, and stagnation. We will eat together, talk together, make each other laugh, and publish articles and books about the benefits of the geezer commune.

We'll be part of a revolution and commandeer the increasingly huge and powerful AARP to demand tax incentives for collective housing. We'll set up a website for housemate matching and offer dispute-resolution services when arguments between housemates get out of hand.

As I see it, the only serious obstacle to this setup is crabbiness. After fifty years of arranging furniture to our own liking, it won't be easy reaching consensus about where to put the electric keyboard and the trampoline, or how to plan meals around one person's dislike of tomatoes. It won't all be cocktails and canasta.

Even so, I'm hoping that as the path through the python gets narrower, it's going to matter less and less who ate the last Oreo. And may we all find the comfort and warmth we need within our gray and wrinkled elephant hide, as we travel through the twilight and into the night.

HOME FOR
THE SOUL

JUDAISM is my journey as well as my home, my headache as well as my heart's ease. It's also been a major part of my livelihood, as I've written Jewish life-cycle books and lectured about Jewish practice all over the United States.

My Jewishness is an essential lens through which I understand myself and my place in the world. And yet, Judaism is an ongoing act of self-invention because I live in a world filled with choices, and because I am a woman from a tradition that would not accept my grandmother's testimony in a court of law.

My religious tradition is a splash of cold water as much as a warm, soothing bath. It keeps me awake, day by day, to the miracles that surround me, to the injustices that require my attention, and to the possibilities of holiness in the world.

ALEPH-BET

I NEED A T-SHIRT that says, "Don't assume that I can read Hebrew."

The fact that I cannot read Hebrew puts me squarely among the silent majority of American Jews for whom the ancient language is a struggle, if not an obstacle. For me, it's also a queen-size embarrassment. After all, I've written six books about Jewish practice and one novel based on a Bible story. People expect me to know the language. *I* expect me to know it.

I do have some prayers memorized (mostly ones attached to melodies), and having taken three Introduction to Hebrew courses, I can follow the letters. Using my finger. If the congregation isn't going too fast.

I've got a familiar and perfectly honorable excuse for my illiteracy: I was not exposed to Hebrew as a child, which is when language acquisition is as natural as growing teeth. I was in my thirties the first time I attempted a class. The teacher was good and the curriculum excellent, but the aleph-bet made me feel like I was banging my head against algebra, and I cannot begin to tell you how much I hated algebra. However, unlike advanced mathematics, I actually need Hebrew.

I haven't given up. I will take another course. I will crack the code and read without sputtering. I've watched other ex-illiterates—including septuagenarians—learn enough to read aloud from the Torah in the presence of four hundred people on Rosh Hashanah. I envy them and anticipate the sense of mastery that comes with that milestone, knowing full well that it denotes merely a technical competence.

I have enough of a Hebrew vocabulary to appreciate the complexity of this language so full of music I will never hear. I grieve for my own tone deafness because I believe that, in some fundamental way, Judaism is not divisible from the sounds and shapes of its elegant letters and sacred texts. Hebrew is essential and central.

And yet, Hebrew is not the whole story. Judaism owes its survival to translation and to transformations dreamed up in other tongues. The Jewish canon and the Jewish soul have been nurtured by Spanish and Ladino, Yiddish and German, and my own beloved English.

I will probably always feel a little embarrassed about whatever level of Hebrew literacy I attain. But I am also fiercely proud of Judaism's democratic insistence that justice is required for all people, that peace should be a portion shared by everyone, and that God is the God of all people, and certainly not just those who read Hebrew.

REFORMING

WHENEVER I'M INVITED to lecture for Jewish organizations, I am asked about my beliefs and opinions. And if it wasn't mentioned when I was introduced to the audience, someone will ask about my affiliation.

I tend to describe myself generically as a "liberal" Jew, which is only a way of saying that I am not an Orthodox Jew. But that answer is a little bit like saying "the Western Hemisphere" when asked, "Where were you born?"

I am proud to belong to a Reform congregation, but when I announce my denominational address, I know that someone is going to grimace as though a plate of ripe Gorgonzola cheese has just been served.

Not all Reform-bashing is so subtle. A few years back, a December issue of *The New Yorker* included a cartoon depicting the holiday "devolution" of rabbis: from Orthodox (bearded and venerable), to Conservative (yarmulke-wearing and mild), to Reform (in a Santa hat).

And then there's the Joke: A guy goes to an Orthodox rabbi and asks him to make a *b'racha* (blessing) on his new Porsche. The rabbi says, "What's a Porsche?" So the new car owner goes to a Conservative rabbi, who says he'll have to convene a rabbinic council to debate the legal precedents that might bear upon such a request. Finally, the man goes to a Reform rabbi, who asks, "What's a *b'racha*?"

The gist is that Reform Jews are assimilated, illiterate, and a half-step away from Unitarianism. In some Jewish fundamentalist quarters, the Reform movement is treated not merely as a joke, but as a mortal threat to Jewish survival.

Enough already! The gibes and insults are simply out of touch with the reality of the largest and fastest-growing Jewish denomination in North America. Reform Judaism is not what it used to be—which is rather the whole point of Reform—and far too vital and varied to squeeze into a sound bite. There are still some Reform temples where no one wears prayer shawls and Hebrew is as foreign as Greek. And there are Reform congregations where the kitchen is kosher and Torah study is a passion. Some Reform temples hold services only when there's a bar mitzvah. Others have daily services, morning and evening.

It's true that some Reform Jews know next to nothing about the texts and traditions of Judaism, but ours are by no means the only members of the tribe in need of remedial education. And we are the hands-down leaders when it comes to new curricula for learners of all ages, and in providing assistance to synagogues that want to improve the ways they teach and serve and support their congregants. To our credit, we are also mavens of self-doubt. We worry about the quality and nature of our Jewish choices, we fret about the authenticity of our decisions, and we debate it all, endlessly.

This makes us an easy target. But ultimately, the willingness to examine and reframe practices and institutions is one of Reform's most endearing and redeeming traits. That, and our trademark insistence upon the centrality of Judaism's prophetic faith that the world can be—indeed, must be—repaired and made whole for all the peoples of the planet.

Rabbi Nachman of Bratslav (1772–1810) declared, "It is forbidden to despair." Hope—no less than monotheism itself—is a normative and non-negotiable pillar of the Jewish mandate. This is a remarkable challenge given the bloody history and embattled state of the Jewish people, but there is no way we can lay that burden down and remain Jews.

Emily Dickinson wrote that hope is the thing with feathers. In the twenty-first century, hope is the thing with muscles. And allies. Keeping despair at bay takes more than individual willpower or spiritual resolve; it requires effort and partners and platforms and committees and faith communities and movements. Your movement. My movement. None is expendable.

Reform Jews do the spiritual, social, and political work of hope—and all the arguing that goes along with it— out in plain sight. Sometimes we're terrific, sometimes we're way off the mark, but we know that we're not free to stop.

Hope is a reliable and consistent plank in the Reform movement's always-under-construction platform. Because "Reform" is not an adjective but a verb. A striving, sweaty, smiling verb.

MY TEACHER

JIM AND I FOUND our congregational home at Beth El (in English: "House of God") when it was Larry Kushner's pulpit. He was Jim's first rabbi. He is the rabbi who changed my life.

Rabbi Lawrence Kushner taught me that "liberal Jewish piety" is not a contradiction in terms. He introduced me to the imaginative form of biblical commentary called midrash. He led me to understand the sanctity of laughter, the possibilities of *halachah* (Jewish religious law), the value of community. Rabbi Kushner showed me that in order to be a serious Jew, I do not have to be a scholar—only a student. And he introduced me to many other wonderful teachers.

The Hebrew word "rabbi" means "teacher." For much of Jewish history, when someone said, "He is my teacher," he was very nearly genuflecting. To call someone "my teacher" was to hint at a relationship of intimate and ultimate importance. It meant, "I would not be who I am were it not for what I learned from this person." It meant, "I am proud of the part of me that was influenced by this teacher." The Talmud goes so far as to say, "He who teaches a person, it is as if he had created him."

Teachers no longer enjoy this kind of esteem. "Teacher" is a word without much clout or mystique in America, Jewish Americans included. Compare the impact of "my daughter the teacher" with "my daughter the surgeon," or "my daughter the assistant district attorney," or "my daughter the concert pianist."

This is not just a matter of status. Do you have any idea how poorly your child's religious-school teachers are getting paid?

But money is not the only reason "my son the rabbi" sounds one thousand percent more impressive than "my son the teacher." Although the word "rabbi" replaced "priest" among Jews a few thousand years ago, the ancient mystique survives. While we no longer want the fancy costumes, sharp knives, and roaring fires of the old Temple priesthood, we still consider our religious leaders a breed apart: not only more pious and closer to God, but also able to counsel the bereaved, preach brilliantly, fight against injustice, raise vast amounts of money, and leap tall buildings in a single bound.

My rabbi, Lawrence Kushner, does some of these things better than others. Leaping is not his strong suit, but he is one of the master teachers of his generation. And I got to sit in his classroom for many years.

There are at least a dozen people about whom I now say, "He is my rabbi," and "She is my rabbi." One of them is Rabbi Kushner's daughter. Another is his successor at Beth El.

There will always be room for new rabbis in my life, and I look forward to learning from each of them. And yet, every new teacher makes me think back to the beginning of this journey, and the bearded, balding man who took me by the hand and said, "Walk this way."

JOYFUL NOISE

FROM DAILY DEVOTIONS to festival services, most of Jewish liturgy is set to music—traditional melodies called *nusach*. Which means that for the most part, it is the cantor rather than the rabbi who leads the congregation in prayer.

My cantor has a lovely voice: clear, powerful, and sweet. But my cantor sings with her teeth, too. And with her hair and her shoes. She sings with a smile of transparent joy, and the sincerity of her prayer dazzles everyone who sees and hears her. When she sings, the atheists smile and sigh.

Even so, the congregation rarely stops to marvel at her talent or technique because she rarely "performs." She and the rabbi do not lead services from up high on the *bimah* (platform); they are down on the floor with the rest of us. And they make sure that we all sing.

My cantor teaches us wordless melodies—*niggunim*—as well as chants, rounds, Sephardic tunes, Hassidic melodies, pieces from the classical Reform choral repertory, contemporary compositions that sound ancient or like American folk songs. She hands out slips of paper with lyrics in Hebrew and English, and when we open our mouths, her face registers delight. When we fill the room with harmony, her smile hits the high beams and we feel like angels singing, "Holy, Holy, Holy."

I am not exaggerating. I swear.

My cantor, Lorel Zar-Kessler, is embarrassed by public and effusive praise. I'm sorry to make her blush, but I see no reason to abide by the tradition of Jewish reticence about music and musicians.

Christians are not bashful about the importance of music in religious life. There is no shame in saying that you chose your church, at least in part, because of a glorious organist or a masterful choir director. And why should there be? Music can be transforming, transfixing, transcendent. It can break your heart and it can heal you.

Jews are a little suspicious of sacred music, a wariness that may date all the way back to the biblical distrust of idolatry. Of all the old gods, only art retains its power to seduce the soul. For many people—including lots of Jews—music is their only spiritual home, Symphony Hall their only sanctuary.

Music speaks to the spirit unmediated. Its magic is undeniable, which was why the ancient priests harnessed it to the service of God. The Temple in Jerusalem echoed with the sounds of horns, drums, bells, and voices singing "Hallelujah." Psalm 150 is unequivocal: Let everything that has breath praise God. With the blast of the horn, with psaltery and with harp, with the timbrel and with dance, with strings and pipes and clanging cymbals. Talk about your joyful noise.

After the Temple's destruction, the song was muted but never stilled. The Torah itself is a libretto whose words are meant to be chanted, not merely read. As lovely as the letters are on the page, when they are married to melody they have the power to reshape the whole universe, atom by atom, breath by breath. Especially when it's my cantor doing the singing.

MEETING ADJOURNED

IT'S NOT ALL APPLES and honey at the House of God, which is, of course, a house of men and women doing the best they can.

Beth El can drive me nuts and break my heart, which is why I try to keep clear of congregational politics. When asked to serve on the board of directors I declined, explaining, "I lack the meeting gene." I am grateful to those who are congenitally able to plan, discuss, hash out, mull, and deliberate, because I can't.

I am not a slacker: I bake cookies, I write brochures, but meetings transform me into a seething misanthrope with violent tendencies. I want to punch anyone who talks too much, even if I agree with what he's saying. I want to shout obscenities at the chair, even if she's my best friend. I do not like the person I become in meetings, which is why I'm so good at saying no when asked to do anything that requires attendance at them.

But sometimes I get a call I can't refuse: "There's going to be a congregational meeting to make an important decision. Every vote counts. Blah, blah, blah." No one has to come right out and tell me to just suck it up and be there. If I don't show my face, I would be abdicating my responsibility, and proving myself lazy and selfish to boot. Guilt does have its uses. So I sit near the back door so I can hit the water fountain at will and try not to get furious at my fellow congregants if and when they start treating each other like relatives.

At big meetings, you really get to see how a congregation functions like an extended family, complete with pompous uncles and long-suffering aunts, Pollyannaish cousins and whiny younger siblings. There's nothing new in these power struggles, personality conflicts, or bad blood. The Bible is full of famous grudge-bearers and illustrious liars, not to mention adulterers and fratricides.

It comes as no surprise that the nastiness quotient rises when money is on the agenda, but I'm perennially stunned at the thoughtless and ugly things people are capable of saying. After one bitter exchange, a friend turned to me and asked, "Am I supposed to kiss that man 'Good Shabbos' next Friday night?"

It's not always a nightmare. Good behavior prevails— more often than not as the congregation matures and learns from our mistakes. Thank heaven.

Unlike a biological family, congregational membership is voluntary, which is why churches and temples splinter and why there are reformations, multiple denominations, and an alternative worship service in many a synagogue library. In other words, I can always throw up my hands and go somewhere else, but that would only mean I'd have to find myself a parallel universe with its own cast of characters and confrontations. So Beth El will remain my spiritual home, my sacred mess. Meetings and all.

MIDRASH — OR NOT

IN 1997 I PUBLISHED a novel that retells the obscure and cryptic biblical tale of Dinah, daughter of Jacob and Leah. I filled in a lot of the details barely hinted at in Genesis 34. I made things up. I changed the narrative both substantially and subtly to suit the needs of my story.

During the three years it took to write and research the food, clothes, midwifery, family arrangements, and funeral customs of the ancient Near East, I thought I was writing historical fiction. But from the moment *The Red Tent* was published, Jewish readers and writers labeled it "midrash."

The word means "to search out" and refers to an ancient, imaginative form of biblical commentary—much of it written in the form of sermons. The rabbis who created this literature (400–1200 C.E.) were seeking to resolve inconsistencies and solve mysteries in the Torah—the first five books of the Hebrew Bible. They filled in the blank spaces between the written words, not primarily to entertain their audiences, but to support the divine authority of the text. That's why the rabbis created ingenious tales that explain why Abraham abandoned his father's ways and set off on his own; what transpired between Cain and Abel before the first biblical murder; why Moses was not permitted to set foot in the Promised Land. These tales, often wildly inventive, sometimes took on a life of their own; a few have even assumed the authority of the Torah itself.

Midrash was once the sole purview of rabbis and scholars, but it's broken loose from its traditional moorings and become a populist tool and a creative doorway into sacred texts. It is sometimes described as a mirror in which regular Jews may find themselves in Torah, a notion not so far removed from the classical purpose of midrash, which was to bind oneself ever closer to God's word.

But midrash has gone much farther afield. I've heard people call the movie *Shakespeare in Love* a midrash on the Bard of Avon's work. In a book about Mary, mother of Jesus, a Catholic feminist described the extra-scriptural stories attached to Mary (such as her immaculate conception and assumption into heaven) as midrash, too.

Given the loosey-goosey use of the word, I've got to wonder what midrash has come to mean. Is any kind of improvisation on classical themes a midrash? Is it midrash if I insert new characters into the biblical tale? Was the animated film *Prince of Egypt* a midrash, or a cartoon, or a cartoon of a midrash?

Most Jewish readers dismiss my misgivings. Some tell me that, after reading *The Red Tent*, they can finally remember who's who in Genesis. Some have said I redeemed their daughter's name—Leah as well as Dinah.

Saying I didn't write *The Red Tent* as Bible commentary does not satisfy Jews or Christians who are furious at me, like the reader who concluded his review on Amazon.com by writing, "My only dilemma is to what to do with this book. . . . I shudder to donate it to the library, lest someone else be inspired by such desecration. Well, trash day is Wednesday."

According to one definition, a midrash is any story that answers a question posed in the Torah. One reader told me that because *The Red Tent* explained why the Egyptian midwives refused to kill the Hebrew babies, it was midrash.

So does function define the form? And who decides what is midrash and what isn't? Would the rabbis who wrote *Midrash Rabbah*, the great classical compendium of the form, recognize *The Red Tent* as midrash? Would their answer make any difference to a contemporary Jew who is convinced that's what it is?

Some Jews have come up with the category "modern midrash" to distinguish *The Red Tent* and other contemporary works from the rabbinic commentaries of the past.

Is modern midrash a whole new food group, or just watered-down soup?

Right there on the cover it says, "A novel." But I'm ready to stop arguing. *The Red Tent* may have come out of my head, but it's out of my hands.

LIVING WATERS

Mikveh, or *mikvah:* (Hebrew. Collection [of water]) Pool of living water. Immersion in a mikveh renders ritually pure a person who has become ritually impure; immersion is also a way to signify a change of status, i.e.: from unmarried to married; from non-Jewish to Jewish. Also the building that houses such a pool.

I WANT A MIKVEH. Not my own, personal mikveh in the backyard, but a community mikveh that I can call my own. There are, of course, mikva'ot (plural) in Boston. I went to one as a bride because I was planning to write a book about

Jewish weddings and I thought I ought to have that traditional experience under my belt, if only for research purposes. I was there once before that, as well, for the conversion of my groom.

But it was at another conversion a few years later that I understood why that particular mikveh could not be "mine." It was during the two hours set aside for liberal conversions every week, and there was a line out the door. A dozen men, women, and children spilled down the stairs and onto the walkway. In a way, it was inspiring to see so many people waiting, wanting to become Jews. But it was hot in the sun, and the mikveh is no place for a queue.

The mikveh should be a place for reflection and celebration, but there was no time, that day, for any of those people to meditate or sing. There was nowhere and no way for the assembled rabbis to lead each of those new Jews through a thoughtful, personal ritual. And afterward, there was nothing to do but get back in the car. As if it were no big deal to change your identity, alter your family constellation, and transform the Jewish people forever.

Those new Jews deserved something better than a line out the door and a handshake. What they got was not a welcome; it was a *shondeh*—the Yiddish word for shame.

I want a mikveh where converts will linger at the mirror, before and after the blessings and immersions that symbolically transform them from not-Jewish to Jewish. In my mikveh, there will be a gracious room for songs and blessings, for hugs and champagne, for gifts of books and candles.

My mikveh will provide liberal time and space for savoring beginnings. Brides and grooms (gay and straight) will come, separately, in preparation for marriage. Setting aside the lists, and plans, and the rush, each will read a poem or a psalm. Forgetting the family pressures for a moment, each will take a leisurely shower. Letting go of the rest, each will walk down the seven stairs into the small pool of water (about the size of a hot tub), immerse, say the blessings, and emerge bearing a new title: "bride" or "groom." Then, out into a gracious parlor for the celebration with gifts and songs, henna and chocolate, voices of joy and gladness.

There will be sad days at my mikveh, too, which will become a safe and healing place for tears, a destination to refresh the soul after divorce, or chemotherapy, or pregnancy loss. Rabbis and social workers will learn the ways water can soothe and calm and denote endings/beginnings for those in pain. It will be a fountain for beginnings.

I want a mikveh where Jews can physically enact the profound process of *teshuvah*—of turning toward God—in the days prior to Yom Kippur, the Day of Atonement. Where rabbis can reflect after burying the dead. Where mourners can mark the slow progress through months and years of bereavement.

The mikveh is most closely associated with monthly use by married women and most mikva'ot are utilitarian structures built by and for the Orthodox community so that wives can immerse themselves according to laws that regulate sexual availability. The monthly immersion was one of the three sacred obligations (mitzvot) required of Jewish women, but it was abandoned by the vast majority of our grandmothers, who thought it demeaning or simply irrelevant.

We Jewish women have long since transformed ourselves into a learned, curious, and creative force in the world; and from this twenty-first-century vantage point, monthly mikveh use is a topic of study, experimentation, and spiritual exploration. After all, at its source, the purpose of regular mikveh visits is to link sex and the sacred, a startling and powerful notion in a world where sex is more commodity than sacrament.

In my mikveh, women will find new ways to celebrate all the unheralded passages of their bodies as they see fit: menarche, the beginning of sex for procreation, the end of nursing, menopause, the attainment of seventy years. The burgeoning community of learned-and-learning Jewish women will decide how the water might sacralize their sexuality. But not only women.

I want to create a mikveh that will be as familiar to male users as to female. Men suffer losses and celebrate milestones deserving of rituals and blessings. In some Orthodox circles, men commonly visit the mikveh for healing—a well-kept secret that needs to be told.

In my mikveh, the "mikveh lady"—a nearly mythic creature believed to be descended from the dragon—will become an educator who teaches all kinds of Jews about how to enter the waters of tradition and plumb possibilities of meaning in them.

At my mikveh, teachers will lead tours for bar and bat mitzvah students, for classes of prospective converts and their families, and for delegations from distant cities who will fly in to see ancient waters flowing into a reimagined vessel within a radically reconstituted Jewish institution. Because this will be a mikveh the like of which has never been seen in Jewish history. Non-Jewish neighbors will be welcome, too, to tour and learn and participate in interfaith conversations about water rituals in our different traditions.

My mikveh must be kosher, with shape, size, and plumbing specifications right out of the Talmud. And it must also be a mikveh that honors the rabbinic mandate for making Jewish life as beautiful as God made the rivers and the lakes.

The water in the mikveh is not "holy water." It is not blessed by rabbis or purified by sages. Nearly all of the required two hundred gallons comes straight from the tap. It is the addition of a symbolic splash of "living water"—such as rainwater—that transforms the municipal supply into something else: a religious wellspring fed by the same headwaters that flowed through Eden in the beginning, when God hovered over the face of the deep.

God divided the waters below from the waters above and it was famously good. It is the same good water that nurtures and sustains the ongoing miracles of creation, from the amniotic sac, to the invisible transport of blood and lymph, to the powerful energies of tides and clouds feeding the planet. All of it sacred: the shower, the kiss, the tear, the flow, the nearly liquid body. Every drop sacred.

I want a mikveh that is as nourishing as the rain, inspiring as the ocean, sweet as childhood swims in the pond. You know that feeling: satisfying, complete, delicious. It is the embrace of a headfirst dive into a perfectly temperate blue pool, into the beginning of all beginnings. And when you surface, the one word on your wet lips is: Ahh. Or, perhaps, Ah-men.

COMMUNITY

IT TOOK ME a lot of years as a temple member before I finally began to understand the meaning of the word "community."

Gauzy with nostalgia, the term seems a setup for disappointment, based on the idea that community is something we lost long ago, back in the "good old days," which occurred (take your pick) in the suburbs of the 1950s, when women chatted over the back fence; or in the old neighborhood, where people schmoozed over the pickle barrels; or in the shtetl, where Jews behaved like Tevye and Golde in *Fiddler on the Roof.*

I have never pined for any historic period prior to the

advent of indoor plumbing, antibiotics, and reliable birth control. Even so, a sepia-tone vision of community has its attractions. Who doesn't long for a place where everybody knows your name?

But that's not what community is all about. I don't know everyone's name at Congregation Beth El of the Sudbury River Valley. Hell, I don't even know the names of some people whose faces I've been looking at for twenty years, people who smile at me and say, "Hi, Anita. How's Jim?"

I say, "Hi," and struggle to remember. Is it Becky? Or Fruma? Or Lucille?

Never mind. I know this woman. I remember when her six-foot-tall high school senior was a goofy seven-year-old, and the Purim she wore a costume made out of two bathroom rugs, and I remember the week her father died. She's the one with the obnoxious Republican husband, I think. Or maybe that's Sarah—or is it Suzanne?

Community is the place with dozens of familiar faces (some with names attached) that always smile back. It is where I am told what a great kid I have by strangers and comforted on the anniversary of my father's death by acquaintances. It is where I feel connected to people I don't even like, but who are part of my life by virtue of membership and affiliation and accident.

Sometimes it's a royal pain (Meetings! Dues! Politics!), but without a communal circle (remember the Venn diagram?) even the fondest family can become claustrophobic. A community consists of many degrees of intimacy, and the cooler ones are just as essential and precious as the fast friendships.

One Friday night at a typical Oneg Shabbat—a nearly sacramental sharing of decaffeinated coffee, cookies, and nontoxic gossip after Friday-night services—I was chatting with Andy, a fellow member and pal about whom I do remember the basics: married to Karen (yeah, I'm sure), father of three, a psychiatrist with an impressive CV.

We were talking about the weather, probably, when one of us (I think it was him) remarked on a story in the day's newspaper predicting an impending epidemic of depression. "So, Doctor," I asked. "How do we protect ourselves?"

He waved his hand at the scene around us. People chatted in twos and threes, a group stood over the dessert table debating the relative merits of brownies versus lemon squares, a bunch of kids played tag in the sanctuary, awake long past their bedtimes. A burst of laughter rose above the general din.

"This," said the doctor. "This is the way we protect ourselves."

ACKNOWLEDGMENTS

In 1979, Ande Zellman was the editor of the *Boston Phoenix* "Lifestyles" section and I was the new hire in the newsroom, occupying the traditional entry-level position for women at the weekly. As assistant to the editor, I answered the phone, filed photographs, kept track of the writers' copy, and, in my spare time, worked as a kind of in-house freelance writer.

One day, Ande invited me to join her for lunch at the Thai restaurant across the street. She likes to tell the story about how, over plates of pad Thai, she realized she'd never met anyone with so many opinions. Soon after, Ande hired me to write a weekly column, which appeared in the

Phoenix for nearly five years. In 1988, when Ande was editor of the *Boston Globe Sunday Magazine,* she offered me the opportunity to opine in those glossier pages; a great many of the essays in this book hail from our collaboration there.

More than any editor I ever met, Ande Zellman encouraged me to take risks. I was buoyed and inspired by her unflagging confidence in my abilities to jump off tall buildings, and to say what I thought even before I was sure I had anything worth saying.

Ande is also the source of my favorite piece of advice regarding writer's block. Whenever I kvetched about being stuck or about having nothing original to say, she'd reassure me with the words, "You're sitting on your brains. Go take a walk."

So I walked, and it helped. What helped even more was talking to Ande, in her office—filled with her enormous, international collection of snow globes—or over Vietnamese soup in her latest "best" Dorchester storefront eatery, or even on the phone. We hashed out the issue, the story, the insight, the problem, the opening paragraph, the big finish. It was a joy reuniting with her to work on this collection.

Ande Zellman is one of many newspaper, magazine, and website editors and copyeditors whose suggestions and saves have been important to my writing over the years. Thanks also to Yossi Abramowitz, Betsy Buffington Bates, Janice Brand, David Cohen, Cynthia Dockrell, Ronnie Friedland, Jeffrey Ganz, Richard Gaines, Rachael Grossman, Vicki Hengen, Fiona Luis, Julie Michaels, Elissa Rabellino, Elaine Ray, David Rosenbaum, Bob Sales, Sharon Slodky, Susan Steinway, Barbara Wallraff, Louisa Williams, and John Yemma. (My apologies for inadvertent omissions.)

Amy Hoffman, E. J. Graff, Aliza Kline, Valerie Monroe, Ed Myers, and Rabbi Barbara Penzner provided assistance and support on this collection. Kudos to Jane Aransky, Anne Frisoli, Mitchell Geller, and Silva Soukiasian for making me look good. Thanks, Emilia, for help with typing. Nan Graham, Sarah McGrath, and Susan Moldow at Scribner are simply a dream to work with, and I'm forever grateful to Amanda Urban for getting me to them.

Last, first, and always, thanks to my family and my friends, for being such gracious and generous fodder all these years, and for their patience with me.